T0376417

ARTRON ART CENTER / URBANUS

A MECCA WHERE BOOKS

ARE CRAFTED & ENJOYED

MASTERPIECE
SERIES

ARTRON ART CENTER / URBANUS

FOREWORD BY **WEN JIE** | INTERVIEW BY **VLADIMIR BELOGOLOVSKY** | TEXTS BY **MENG YAN**
COMPLETED BUILDING PHOTOGRAPHY BY **ALEX CHAN, ZENG TIANPEI, WU QIWEI, YANG CHAOYING,**
WANG DAYONG, ZOU JIA, CHEN YU

OSCAR RIERA OJEDA
PUBLISHERS

CONTENTS

FOREWORD
BY WAN JIE

Artron Art Center:
Return to the Essence of Artistic Spirit
— Books are never-ending exhibitions.
Every book is a world of art and culture.

— Wan Jie, Artron Art Group

Shenzhen is at the forefront of reform and opening up. It is an expression of the spirit of the Chinese and a testing ground for the Chinese dream. And for me, Artron Art Center is the testing ground of my artistic dream. The Artron Art Center, located in Nanshan District, Shenzhen, is a perfect blending of books and art, presenting an unprecedented artistic and aesthetic complex: a 50x30m wall of books, and a museum-style art bookstore elaborately displayed in the Center, maximizing the reading and aesthetic effects of books.

Twenty-eight years ago, I started my business in Shenzhen and engaged in the traditional industry of printing in such an economically developed area. It was also at that time that I planned Artron's strategic positioning of culture and art. Whatever the level of economic development, it is culture that ultimately records history. As the theme of Artron's corporate video "Resistance to Fade Out" points out, only culture is eternal. Therefore, in the process of marching from traditional industry to the field of culture, we have always adhered to the culture, embraced technology and followed the pace of the market for continuous transformation and upgrading, until we finally became a model for the transformation of Shenzhen enterprises. In my opinion, this is not just the success of Artron, but also the success of culture, which is driven by cultural forces.

Today's China is at a critical stage of economic development and urgently needs to export soft power and show the true image of China. But in the end, it is the achievements in the arts and culture that will be remembered. In this process, cultural enterprises have great opportunities and responsibilities to contribute cultural soft power, which is why I created a complex for inheriting, preserving and promoting culture. Since the founding of Artron, I've always believed that Artron needs to learn from the best art resources in the world and bring them together to form a force in this digital age. Therefore, it is important to understand, respect and learn from other cultures, as well as to introduce and learn from excellent foreign experiences. Our parents didn't have such systematic learning opportunities, so Artron has been committed to building a large art database for more people to improve their artistic culture and taste, stimulate their artistic creativity, ex-

WAN JIE, born in Beijing in 1962, is the founder and Chairman of Artron Art Group. He served as a Ph.D. adviser at the Chinese National Academy of Arts, a Vice-president of the Copyright Society of China, a Vice-chairman of the China Committee of Corporate Citizenship, an initiator and director of the Forbidden City Cultural Heritage Conservation Foundation, a director and primary Vice-president of the Society of Entrepreneurs & Ecology, a director of the China Song Ching Ling Foundation and the Taofen Fund, the President of the Young Curators Foundation of the Wu Zuoren International Foundation of Fine Arts and an initiator of the Shenzhen Mangrove Wetlands Conservation Foundation.

He was included in the "Four Groups" members of national publicity and culture system authorized by the Department of Publicity of CPC Central Committee in 2009. He has won the titles as "Top 100 Publishers and Outstanding Entrepreneurs at the 60th Anniversary of New China", "CCTV China's Annual Economic Figures 2008", "Chinese Culture Figures 2012" and "Annual Figures of China's Cultural Industry 2012".

He is a member of the CPPCC (circle of press and publishing), and a member of the China Democratic League Central Committee, a Vice-director of its Culture Commission and a standing director of its Academy of Fine Arts, and a Vice-director of the China Democratic League Shenzhen Committee.

pression and emotion, and pass these cultural and artistic resources to future generations.

I'm a bit of a book lover. Traditional printing has a great contribution to the inheritance of culture. Books are expressions of human emotions and carriers of cultural memory, and some treasured books themselves are luxurious works of art. I had a vision from a long time ago that I wanted to create an art center with books as the bond and a monumental building with books. Therefore, I put all my efforts into Artron to integrate art resources. With the ancient library and the information technology that Artron has always been good at, I brought good technology experience to the audience and created such a compound as Artron Art Center, an aesthetic complex.

Artron Wall is not only a window, it is facing the world, a milestone, an innovative exploration of books, but also a return to the essence of art spirit. The Art Center has a rich and in-depth collection of books from all over the world, which is a feat worthy of inheritance and continuation, and more importantly, an expression of a magnificent career. Different from traditional bookstores, Artron's art platform comprehensive service resources are thorough and complete, providing inherently excellent conditions for creating an art complex with a new concept.

I hope Artron Art Center has the specifications of a museum in space design. The function of art collection is also the function of museum collection. Here, books no longer have the same meaning as traditional books but exist as treasures and collectibles. The significance of books as luxury goods and treasures is the need to return to the spirit of art itself. I want readers to appreciate a book as a work of art when they read it. Books are the knowledge and cultivation of beauty. Today, much of the information we are exposed to through electronic media is fragmented, and more and more people are trying to break the form. Bookstores don't have a fixed form, and many people are looking for the future business form of bookstores. The same is true for the publishing industry, which will be more diverse in the future and may take many forms.

In this digital world, books have changed dramatically. They are works of art, never-ending exhibitions, and collectibles. Paper books have a sense of memory, history, ritual and a sense of vicissitudes on touch. Books are a kind of decoration but also the gift of cultural exchange, and they may become more and more precious in the future. It's actually a spiritual luxury.

Every book in the Artron Art Center is a world of culture and art. It is the great wish of Artron and also my dream to let more people get aesthetic and artistic edification from art and books while remembering history.

The Artron Art Center Program

The Artron Art Group:
conveying the beauty of art through technology

Taking a craft approach to art data and digital technology, Artron Art Group creates platforms that bring the different stages of art production together, developing essential products, services and experiences for the art community and its public under a philosophy of "serving people with art" by "serving the people's art". It is the group's mission to promote, share and enhance the value of art.

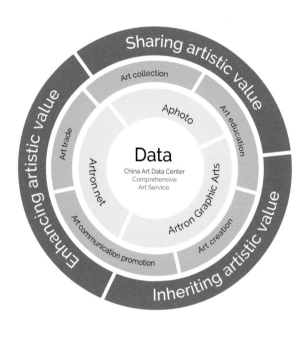

1 Artron Graphic Arts
- Professional Art Book Printing
- Creative Design and Quality Planning
- Quality Print-On-Demand Customization

2 Aphoto
- Optimal solutions for photography afficionados
- Photo+solution for the Cultural Tourism Industry
- Photo+solution for individual consumption

3 Artron.net
- Database and application
- Database of Chinese Artwork
- Art Market Price Index Artbase, Cloud
- Service for Artists
- Art Trading
- Artplus
- On-line auction
- Integrated services for the art industry
- Artwork Digitized and application
- Artwork Authentication

INTERVIEW
BY VLADIMIR BELOGOLOVSKY

"Our Battlefield is in the City"
In conversation with Meng Yan
By Vladimir Belogolovsky
April 26, 2021

Vladimir Belogolovsky: Could you talk about how you came across architecture and why you decided to pursue it professionally?

Meng Yan: My high school years were in the early 1980s, which was a time when very few people in China had an idea of what architecture is and what architects do, let alone the concept of modern architectural practice. I initially wanted to study art, as my undergraduate major, but my parents suggested that it would be more "practical" to pursue architecture in terms of getting a decent job. In 1983, I was accepted to the Architecture School at Tsinghua University. In my view, architecture is about doing something positive for people, and to improve their liv-

ing reality. I see architecture as a profession that could bring positive changes.

In the 1970s, the number of new modern buildings in Beijing became noticeable, a strong contrast to old courtyard houses and hutongs. Later on I learned about Liang Sicheng, the famous architectural historian, and father of modern architecture in Chinese education, whose efforts to preserve the ancient parts of Beijing made people conscious about the challenges that the city is facing as it goes through the process of industrialization and modernization.

Growing up in Beijing enabled me to explore the preserved Royal palaces, gardens, and such museums as the Summer Palace and the Forbidden City, from a very young age. While most of the tourists were attracted by the imperial treasures on display, my attention was drawn by the traditional ink and wash paintings and the historical buildings that house them. In the late 1970s I began to study traditional Chinese landscape

VLADIMIR BELOGOLOVSKY (b. 1970, Odessa, Ukraine) is an American curator and critic. He graduated from the Cooper Union School of Architecture in 1996. After practicing architecture for 12 years, he founded his New York-based Curatorial Project, a nonprofit, which focuses on curating and designing architectural exhibitions that have appeared the world over. This work is complemented by lectures and catalog texts. He writes for *Arquitectura Viva* (Madrid) and *SPEECH* (Berlin) and is a columnist on *STIR* and *ArchDaily*. He has interviewed over 350 leading international architects as an ongoing project on issues surrounding individual identities on architecture and has written fifteen books, including *Imagine Buildings Floating Like Clouds!* (Images Publishing, 2022); *Iconic New York* (DOM, 2019); *Conversations with Peter Eisenman* (DOM, 2016); *Conversations with Architects* (DOM, 2015); *Harry Seidler: Lifework* (Rizzoli, 2014); and *Soviet Modernism: 1955-1985* (TATLIN, 2010). Belogolovsky has curated over 50 international exhibitions. They include the Architects' Voices Series (World Tour since 2016), world tours on the work of Emilio Ambasz, Harry Seidler, and an American tour on Colombian architecture. In 2008, he produced the Chess Game exhibition for the Russian Pavilion at the 11th Venice Architecture Biennale. He is an Honorary Professor and Corresponding Member of the International Academy of Architecture in Moscow (IAAM), and IAAM's official emissary in the United States. He has lectured at universities and museums in more than 30 countries. In 2018, at the invitation of Li Xiaodong, Belogolovsky spent the fall semester teaching at Tsinghua University in Beijing as a visiting scholar.

painting; it felt as if the whole new world was unrolled before my eyes. What is crucial to know is that Chinese landscape paintings are not about depicting reality but about conceptualizing one's imagination of landscape as an idea and exploring its possibilities. It is about the landscape created in one's own mind, affected by one's personal experience. I was particularly fascinated by the misty mountains and fairy courts with people in contemplation depicted in paintings of the Song Dynasty…

VB: After earning your bachelor's degree in 1988 you decided to go to graduate school. Could you talk about that experience?

MY: We learned to design all sorts of buildings during our undergraduate years – kindergartens, hotels, stadiums, and culture centers. However, my curiosity about the history of Chinese architecture and the principles of traditional Chinese gardens and paintings was not fulfilled. Continuing into graduate school was a great opportunity for me since it allows free choice of focus. My thesis project was about the Chinese literati garden rooted in Chinese art and culture. While I was working on my thesis, I spent two months traveling and studying Chinese traditional gardens in Suzhou, Hangzhou, and Ningbo which gained me insights about the Chinese literati ideology behind the Chinese gardens.

The decade between 1980 and 1990 was a time of great economic reforms. It was the golden decade for China since it entered an entirely new era. My formative years of learning coincided with it. School doesn't only open windows for observation, but also takes on the role of transitional platform, which allowed me to experience and learn from the drastic changes of all aspects of society.

What was happening outside the campus had a great impact on us students. Apart from the study, we noticed many external influences. We went to art exhibitions and closely followed the literary scene, film, and contemporary art, all of which were emerging then. Everything was accelerated by the great economic reforms promoted by Deng Xiaoping. He went to Shenzhen in 1984 to reaffirm the new economic policy there. We followed those events and gradually our minds were opened. In 1988, I visited Shenzhen for the first time. It was a place where – at that time – everything seemed possible. It felt like witnessing an emergence of modernity in all aspects. People of my age are probably the last generation in China that believed in idealism and social ambition, we had faith in changes that would make society better, and that tomorrow will be better than today.

But after the '90s the whole society shifted towards consumerism. "Time is money" - the propaganda from Shenzhen became people's mantra. Making money became a priority.

VB: After graduation you could have followed many other graduates to get a job at one of the government-run Local Design Institutes, but you decided to continue your studies in the U.S., right?

MY: Before going to the U.S. I worked for a couple of years at a semiprivate architectural office in Beijing; it was collectively owned. It was before private practice was allowed in China. It was a non-hierarchical organization and much more efficient than government-owned design institutes at the time.

VB: How was your experience in the States?

MY: In 1993, I went to Miami University in Oxford, Ohio, and after earning my master's degree there I went to New York City to work. So, I missed the '90s in China almost entirely, which was the time of the "great leap forward" and the process of commercialization and growing individualism. Of course, Ohio and New York were two completely different worlds. Ohio was very quiet, conservative, and slow-paced. My first student project in Ohio was an urban regeneration study in Cincinnati. I analyzed the urban decay, which was hard to understand for someone coming from China where people were everywhere, and cities were constantly expanding. It was the first time that I saw empty sites in the middle of the city, confrontations between blacks and whites. And my thesis project was on history, research, and the regeneration of the Chinatown in Chicago. I was always interested in the social aspects of architecture and wondered how street life and architecture are intertwined. Once I moved to New York, the urban environment was entirely different yet again, as it was all about density, intensity, and verticality. So, for me it was going from one cultural shock to the next – Beijing, Ohio, and then New York. The contrasts were astounding.

VB: In New York you worked at KPF. How was that experience?

MY: Yes, for most of the time. And the main reason was because the office was expanding very quickly as a global practice, particularly into China and East Asia. I spent most of my time working on projects in Shanghai. But the office had nothing in Shenzhen at that time.

Besides work, it was important to be in New York to explore the city saturated with great ideas. All the nutrients are there. We experienced the city by going everywhere on foot and visiting museums and galleries. I love the city because there is so much to be discovered.

VB: At what point did you realize that China presented even bigger opportunities for young architects than the West and that it was time to go back?

MY: You know, many of my friends wanted to stay in the States. In fact, among those Chinese students who went abroad before 1990s, not coming back was the trend. But things started to change; in 1993, Yung Ho Chang went back to Beijing and started his practice, which became the first independent architectural practice in China after the economic reforms. I remember seeing his solo exhibition in New York curated by Hou Hanru, a well-known international curator. For us, that was a great inspiration. Later, we saw the compelling work of Liu Jiakun in Chengdu. So, together with my friends – now partners, Liu Xiaodu and Wang Hui – we were able to sense the new horizon.

VB: And it seems that from the very beginning you envisioned your practice as something quite powerful and urban. You went to Shenzhen where you were looking for challenging opportunities, whereas most other leading architects in China work out of Beijing and Shanghai.

MY: We did not choose Shenzhen. I would say that we were chosen by Shenzhen. We originally planned to start our practice in our hometown Beijing, but at that time Beijing was still very quiet, the excitement of the Beijing Olympics had not arrived yet. As I mentioned, I witnessed the emergence of Shenzhen early on with no more than a dozen skyscrapers. In 1995, I went there again, and I did not see anything that would attract me to stay - it was still a "cultural desert."

Towards the beginning of the new century, after almost 20 years of rapid urbanization, Shenzhen was booming with more challenges and more opportunities. Even though it was still rough and brutal, it started to present potentials like New York City did one hundred years ago. Everyone goes there in order to survive and in the hope of success. Attracted by the opportunities of unprecedented urbanization there, we decided to give Shenzhen a try.

VB: Was moving to Shenzhen, the fastest growing city in the world, about pursuing a particular project or was it your conviction that the city needed architects such as yourself and your partners, Liu Xiaodu and Wang Hui?

MY: It was the other way around – first we got a project and then we moved here. We seized an opportunity to participate in an urban design competition initiated by the city government. It was a major regeneration project and we won a small part of it, a garden. That sparked our enthusiasm, knowing that even people like us who don't have any connections, could win a project in a fair competition and do something for the city. Wang Hui and I were still in New York then, and URBANUS did not exist yet. Liu Xiaodu was traveling back and forth. Once we had the project, we gained confidence and received some recognition. Then, slowly, we began building our practice together.

VB: Let's talk about the Artron Art Center. What was your client's main objective and vision for this project?

MY: Originally, Artron was a print factory; it was well known in the printing industry, but it was something very obscure from the architectural standpoint. It was also going through a major transformation at that time. Our client already positioned the project as a cultural service center when they reached out to us. The Chairman and President of Artron Art Group, Mr. Wan Jie, came to me and said, "We still want it to be a factory, of course, but it should become a hybrid building. We would like it to contain our headquarters, an art center, a library, plus a museum with an extensive collection." They even wanted to add a dormitory for their workers. That was quite an ambition. So, I asked him, "How would you imagine this building to look like? Do you want it as a cluster of buildings, a high-rise, or a monolithic 'object'?" He did not answer this question directly. But he said, "I want this building to look entirely like an art center, not a factory." That was a very clear message to me.

We did a lot of research and made various attempts trying out different schemes on this particularly difficult site, which was at the periphery of the city back then. It was bounded by three highways and was adjacent to a concrete plant. The biggest challenge for us was to make a hybrid building with all the required programs and to transform the image of Artron from being just a factory to a cultural center. To do so requires the building to operate as a space for one-stop printing and cultural services, and to integrate all programs into one single volume.

Besides, our client also suggested that the building would welcome artists to come there to supervise the printing of their monographs, to give lectures, and so on. With the ambition of becoming a major information center, it could potentially grow into the biggest artists' database in China. I could see right away that the mission was to redefine the business model of Artron, and turn it into something new, for which the building itself serves as a broadcast of this ambition.

VB: You said for URBANUS architecture is about finding the right problem and right strategy to solve it. What was your design strategy for Artron? And let's talk about its space organization, programmatic components, and circulation.

MY: It is a tough project because of the collision of its many different components, such as the factory, the headquarters, and ways in which those programs interact with the public zones. It

feels like designing a small city. Thus, it is essential to build up a narrative that connects the individual parts, and to form a dialogue between the building and its surrounding environment. So, the challenge was both from the inside and from the outside.

From the outside, not only was the site a remote place, it was also full of uncertainties because no one could anticipate what was going to happen with the context around it. When you design in a developed city in Europe or North America, you know the context and can produce a particular response. But here we had to "start from scratch" all on our own. We didn't want to do an isolated project that ends up having nothing to do with its surroundings. So, looking around, the only thing that was determined of the site were the highways. We know that people would experience the building by driving past it along these elevated highways at 60 miles per hour, which is very different from what people inside the building would feel.

One unifying element for the project is the vertical library. Spatially it serves as a device to connect all the major programs; it forms a gathering space for the public to enjoy. Initially, our proposal was just a simple lobby, but when Mr. Wan told us that Artron has a collection of over ten thousand books, we thought that the lobby could take on the role of displaying those books like a library. Mr. Wan appreciated the idea of having this "library wall" right in the middle; it turned out to be fifty meters long and four stories high.

VB: So what was initially planned as an active library accessible throughout became a simple display wall?

MY: Absolutely. It was conceived to operate as a vertical urban plaza for a truly interactive experience for the public. The intention was to be able to climb and explore this library wall by walking through it, looking around, and peeking into the production spaces of the factory or other parts of the building. In that way, the library wall would both conceptually and literally function as a connector, instead of a solid element for display. The idea was really to create a public forum in the heart of the building. We also connected the lecture hall with the interior courtyard so that it could form a large outdoor meeting space when the weather is nice. Thus, everyone working in the Artron Art Center would be exposed to the cultural events taking place in what would be transformed into something like a theater.

VB: You compared this building to an urban square. Were you at all influenced by such projects as CCTV by Rem Koolhaas in terms of the building's circulation, a loop of interconnected experiences or a competition project for Eyebeam Museum by Diller Scofidio + Renfro where the museum, theater, education, and production facilities were separated and brought together by an undulating ribbon, a hybrid of floor/wall/ceiling element. They called it "a system of controlled contamination." Could you talk about your main inspirations while planning Artron?

MY: We are certainly well acquainted with these examples, but we wouldn't pursue them as our direct inspirations. I had a chance to visit CCTV during and after its construction, and I like it a lot. Besides its unique geometry, I really appreciate its original intention – to allow public access to penetrate this government-owned institution. This vision helped to unravel the idea of a building as a monumental object and conceive it as series of exploratory experiences. Of course, that's not how it was realized but I admire the proposal.

We discussed our idea with Mr. Wan a lot, and he pushed the need to engage the public in order to make Artron a part of the city not just visually but also experientially, and to turn it into a cultural destination for people to visit on holidays and weekends. This new building typology – a private headquarters to perform public functions – is very attractive to Chinese entrepreneurs. For example, the Vanke Center here in Shenzhen is a successful model showing how businesses could pay back to society.

VB: I spoke to Steven Holl, the architect of the Vanke Center, and he explained that he was commissioned the project without a program. It was his responsibility, as an architect, to design not just the building but its program.

MY: This is true. So many clients in China ask their architects to come up with the program. We just had ten grand cultural buildings competitions finish here in Shenzhen and many of them don't really have a designated program – designing the program is often a part of architectural competitions. I am glad that Artron was different. Our client had a very clear vision, and he was the one who was pushing the architect to respond to it and elaborate it further. Of course, we did go through many discussions, but the objective was well-stated, so a lot of time was spent on coming up with ways of connecting different programs.

VB: You mentioned the influence of Rem Koolhaas on your work. What would you say you learned from him the most?

MY: Rem is one of the greatest thinkers in our profession. What he contributes to the field of architecture is not just his buildings, but particularly his urban agenda. We collaborated on the Cristal Island competition with his office in 2009, and the same year we worked as design consultant with him on West Kowloon Cultural District. You already brought up his CCTV Building, and to me the most extraordinary part of that project is the public loop that engages the people within.

How would you energize a very politically charged and institutional building? Rem undertook similar ideas in his project of the Stock exchange building in Shenzhen, where he incorporated a public square under the elevated podium. Unfortunately, the conceptual approach of both projects was not possible to be fully realized. Still, what I am trying to learn from him is this mode of utopian and idealistic thinking. You may fail to re-

alize it, but at least you must try. Thus, the lesson would be this – how to find balance between the reality and the imagination? And moreover, how could the city be improved?

VB: You said you see every project as an opportunity to understand the city better. In one of your interviews you said, "We need to engage with the city more; I think this is one of the most unique aspects of URBANUS – we actively engage and we promote ourselves not only as architects but also as strategic coordinators and as urban curators. We try to do more." Could you touch on this and on the opportunities that Artron presented to you?

MY: From the very beginning when we started our office about 20 years ago, we have our goal set, which was to engage the city in the architecture that we would create. This particularly applies to the new cities such as Shenzhen where we started. It is rare, here in China, for a design practice to focus on working in a particular city, and many critics say that China is an experimental field for global architects. For us, however, architecture is an urban experiment and Shenzhen is our chosen ground. So, almost all our works are in Shenzhen. I like the idea of always working in a familiar place, and I do think that the architect must be well acquainted with the place where he works. To me, making an interesting piece of architecture is not too difficult, but being able to incorporate ideas rooted in its local culture and to do the "right thing" is very tough, and this, I believe, should really be the most important challenge for any architect. That's why we do a lot of research before making any design decisions. The point is to truly understand the place and the problem.

Artron Center is not our typical project. What we often do is to make architecture that supports urban regeneration, and that helps to revitalize a part of the city. But Artron reflects many of our urban design methods and strategies. For example, we rarely work on projects that start off from a scenic site, and I admire many of our colleagues who work on such places, especially those situated in the countryside or out in nature. In contrast, our sites always begin with an unappealing and unsettling condition, often located on the outskirts of the city – and I am fond of that. When I look at photos of Artron, as an isolated building, I don't think highly of those images. But I really enjoy photos that show the urban settings around it, especially the shots of the building from underneath the highways. I like to see when our buildings are framed or cut by structures and infrastructures around it, and how they merge with these rough environments. That's what Artron is about. Confronting existing conditions and proposing a kind of building that could greatly improve the area is how we always start our projects. All our buildings really came out of their sites – none of them are inserted into the context as a mere beautiful object. What we attempt to do is a kind of superimposition of futuristic thinking over the existing context that needs a new energy source and new connectivity. Our interventions aim at improving energy flows on an urban scale.

VB: If you look at this project in the context of your other projects, do you see it as a link between them or is it a stand-alone solution? How would you compare Artron to your other urban interventions in Shenzhen?

MY: Even though all our projects look very different, the thinking behind Artron and our other projects is very similar. The idea is to infuse transformation, to turn a plain and boring area into a vivid neighborhood and community. For example, take Yuehai Community Culture and Sports Center in Nanshan District in Shenzhen. On a typical uninteresting site, we proposed a vertical stacking of various sports programs with culture, hospitality, and social services – all integrated. This will bring new experiences and positive energy that did not exist there before. And if you go to Artron now, already you will see changes provoked by our building, as new developments are coming up around it. We believe architecture can empower a place and make life more meaningful.

VB: In other words, Artron became a catalyst. To you, architecture is a tool, not simply an aesthetic device. That's what you try to push in your work. You just mentioned that the book wall was originally conceived as a library, but it was not realized that way. Are there any other ideas that failed to materialize?

MY: I would list some of the critical, even fundamental ideas about how the project was imagined in its ideal form. If you look at the original form and many interiors, for the most part, they were executed very closely to how we planned them, even though some of the details were omitted. The library became a book wall. Visually, it may be very close to how it was designed, but the fact that it is not an interactive library is a missed opportunity. The challenge was about how to manage these spaces we imagined, how to operate them, how to deal with the fire code issues, and so on. There are technical constraints that make some ideas quite challenging to execute.

Another challenge was to connect the production space at the factory and the public zones, particularly the museum. It became an operational issue to allow for multi floor open stairs. So, we lost some of these connections even purely visual links through wall apertures. That was unfortunate. Another loss was because we could not carry out the gallery spiral as a singular continuous space. So, it is not about the individual components, it is about maintaining the connectivity throughout the entire building. The original idea was to design a building like a real town that allows you to get to the central square in numerous different ways. Similarly, people would be able to explore the building's core space like a city square. The idea was to create a non-hierarchical building. What we succeeded with is that the building did become a public cultural space and it became an anchor for the area. It now stimulates further development and it clearly added a new layer of public life to this community.

VB: Could you talk about the place of URBANUS as an independent architectural practice in China, especially with regard to your commitment to address urban issues?

MY: It is true that URBANUS works more on large scale urban projects. I think it is about our view of reality, particularly that of Chinese cities. While some would talk about those cities in a very negative way, saying that Chinese cities accumulate "junk buildings," I would say that this issue should be approached from an alternative perspective. We see our city as a battlefield, and we are confronting the city as an "enemy" – we are like "guerrillas" fighting to improve the urban conditions. And even after working in Shenzhen for 20 years, it is still very tough for us. I would encourage more independent architects to help tackle the urban issues beyond the giant corporate institutes. Cities are so complex; there must be many parallel and collective forces to address all the urban issues from many points of view with many alternatives. There is no single strategy. We need diversity in our visions to better address the city in all its corners.

We lived for years in New York City and appreciated its diversity, density, and multiculturalism; we believe that the unique energy of large cities will help them evolve. I also think people who like living in cities are fundamentally different from those who live in the suburbs and the countryside, while the kinds of architecture that we produce in these places are also very different. We need to acknowledge and understand these differences.

VB: And surely these people and the two kinds of architecture can learn from each other and benefit each other.

MY: Absolutely. It is our major preoccupation – how to enjoy living in the city and how to balance between high and low densities. How can we take advantage of complexities out of high density and create situations that are attractive and enjoyable. Cities like New York and Hong Kong serve us as great models. And we want to prove that our architecture can also offer great experience and a great variety of lifestyles and experiences in the middle of a metropolis. Compared to the pure pastoral countryside, a spatially "chaotic" city can be a great thing.

VB: You position your firm in the following way, "URBANUS is more than a design practice, it is a think-tank, an urban curator, and mediator. It aims to formulate architectural strategy from the complexities and uncertainties in contemporary Chinese urbanism." This was stated in one of your lectures. Could you talk about the key intentions of your work? How would you define your focus?

MY: What we try to see in complex and uncertain situations are opportunities. We want to learn from conditions that are seemingly impossible, ugly, and negative. And we want to turn these situations around into something positive. Our practice is more about adding new layers of urban substances. Our focus is to superimpose, to accept what is already there and to improve it. And, of course, we can only add more spaces and containers. But the intention is to bring new programs into our spaces and the entire area. We see each of our projects as a fragment of a much bigger urban fabric. We have been working on various parts of Shenzhen's urban fabric since our first project 21 years ago, and we keep inserting our projects into this fabric, making the city softer, in a way. We add softness to the city.

VB: I like this word softness in relation to the city and the idea of making the city softer. What other single words would you use to describe your work or the kind of architecture you want to achieve?

MY: Intervention. What I really like about architecture is that magic moment when something new gets realized out of somewhere lifeless. When a place is born for public gathering and enjoyment, people's lives there will be different. The idea is to intervene and to weave the urban fabric. We should also think about this not only when we build but also when we take buildings down. Architecture is a lot more complex than just the material and forms. Architecture's interiority is very important. I think architects can learn a lot from doctors – how to identify a problem and find a holistic solution for how to heal it. If there is no problem and you come to an architect to ask for a beautiful building, that's fine, but that's a different story. We are more interested in solving problems. Our clients come to us with difficulties. URBANUS focuses on solving problems, particularly urban problems. Many of our buildings become infrastructures and that's another word that describes our architecture.

VB: What would you say about the state of architecture in China right now and what are your main concerns in the profession today in general?

MY: What concerns me most is not the projects by individual architects but the state and development of Chinese cities. There is a lot of construction going on. Of course, not all of it is bad – there is some progress. Our architecture is becoming more diverse. There are many good buildings being built. But a collection of good buildings will not guarantee a good city. Looking at New York City, you might think that most buildings are in a sense quite "boring," but a lot of times "boring" buildings are the essential ingredients of a great city.

In China, we've been in a kind of World Expo mindset for too long. Clients want their buildings to be special formally and think little about their programs and performance. And, in their minds, "good buildings" are often associated with foreign architects, but those architects often design projects out of how they imagine China instead of the real China. So, when you bring so many different ideas into one place it becomes the World Expo situation, a kind of Las Vegas model without a cohesive urban fabric. So, my concern is not about good-looking buildings but about how to reconnect and improve our cit-

ies. How do we learn from traditional cities that work so well? Though of course, we should never literally model the future after the past.

Most importantly, I would encourage young Chinese architects to stay focused on working in our cities, instead of looking for perfect places to build something that is just pleasing to the eye, which to me is a form of escapism. Architects should be more ambitious both culturally and socially. In the end, architecture is a local practice, we need local architects who understand local places and local people well.

VB: I agree with you and I wish local planners and regional governments would engage talented local architects more actively in working on local urban projects, as they can't compete with Local Design Institutes and foreign architects. In your view, which one building built in China since the beginning of the new century would you nominate as the most important and why?

MY: If I must choose one it would most likely be CCTV. The CCTV building perfectly showcased Beijing with its open gestures and ambition at the time of 2008 Beijing Olympics. Serving complicated broadcasting functions, the building works as a media city that possesses powerful urban quality both inside and outside. Architecturally speaking, it displays great design creativity. By not being the tallest building, it gained a unique shape, that inspires imagination and manifests the ambition of China at that moment. The building is a success in terms of making architecture a part of public awareness. It is the most talked about building in the country. It is both criticized and praised by the public and within the profession. What is unique is that this building, finally, sparked ordinary people's interest and showcased the power of architecture, which is truly remarkable.

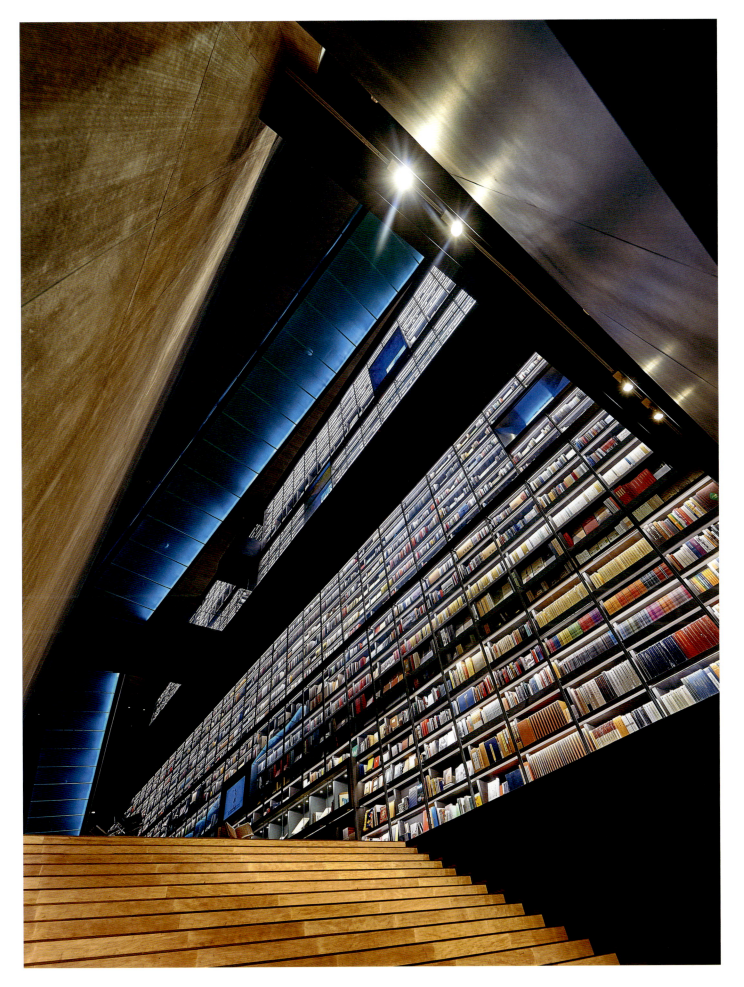

DESIGN

DESCRIPTION

BY MENG YAN

Artron is a leading printing enterprise in China. As the core project of its cultural industry, Artron art net is an important service platform for artist archives. Taking account of this and the fact that the project base is far from the city center, Shenzhen Artron Art Center hopes to become a one-stop printing cultural comprehensive service center. The site is located on the city edge surrounded by three highways. The surroundings are still under construction and full of uncertainties. In order to keep away from the noisy and chaotic environment, the building is idealized to be a landmark to define this area. Since the site adjacent with highways and will only leave a fast image, the building shape should be continuous and integrated with the large-scale urban infrastructure to form a dialogue between the two.

While considering the volume as a whole, the architects must think about the human scale and how to digest this huge volume. On the one hand, on the premise of integrity and continuity, the considerable gaps between different parts of the volumes are created to bring people comfortable experiences with the space. On the other hand, a triangular plot is reserved as a public park on the corner of the site. Observed from the surrounding blocks, the building is different on every side. The façade is combined with external wall tiles and curtain wall. Integrated with the relation between building volumes, the external wall is jointed horizontally and vertically with eight kinds of narrow blue tiles which are varied in density and temperature. This cus-

tomized "Artron blue" echoes the corporation culture, at the same time giving people fresh visual impressions.

The wreathed volume encloses two quiet inner gardens in different heights. Multiple departments placed around the courtyard enjoy perfect ventilation and lighting, and also block the noise from the outside. The gap in the central building volumes makes an elevated platform in the second floor, which allows access to the interlayered multi-function hall through the central grand staircase, forming a semi-outdoor space for various public activities and exhibits. People's activities in the courtyard steps can be seen through the glass window in each floor's office areas, which also creates multi-layered dialogues and communications. Another sky garden with lush bamboos connects the fourth, fifth, and sixth floor's workshops, art gallery and the head office. Inside the building, the vertical space which crosses four floors between offices and workshops is designed as a library for collecting and displaying Artron's increasing book collection. An open staircase folding through the whole space connects different floors, and together with the people walking through it, creates the most dramatic moment within this building. Isolated from the public functions, the art gallery is placed in parallel with the corporate headquarters and independently suspends in the top floor with the best view, creating various possible inner visiting paths. Different functions are overlaid, interconnected and mixed inside the whole building, just like a micro three-dimensional urban cluster.

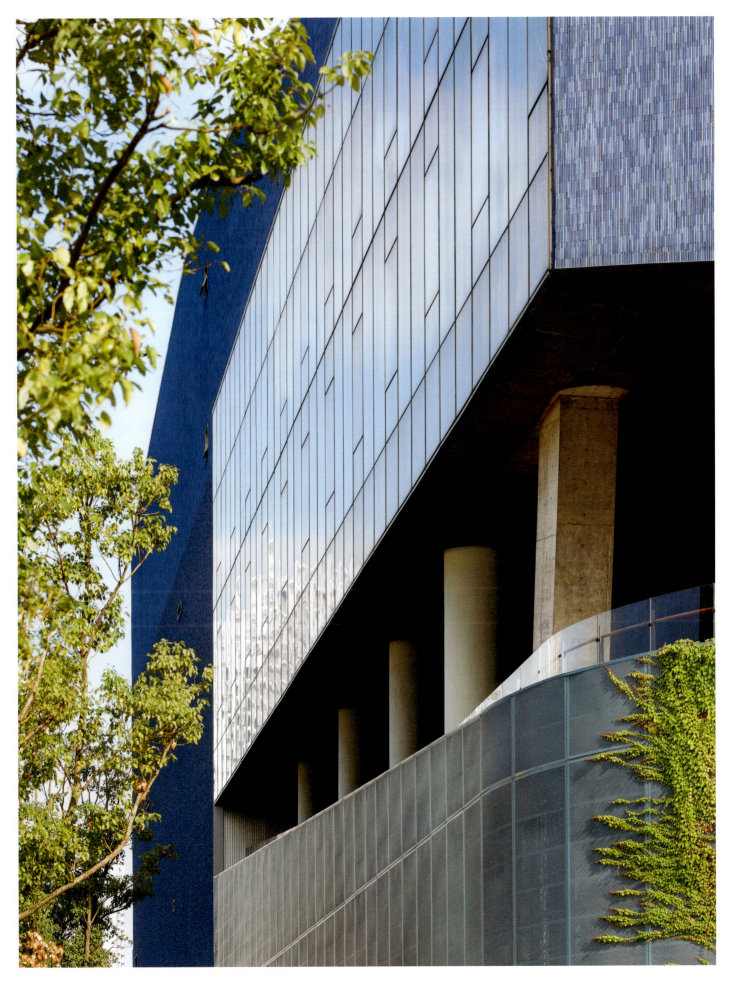

SKETCHES

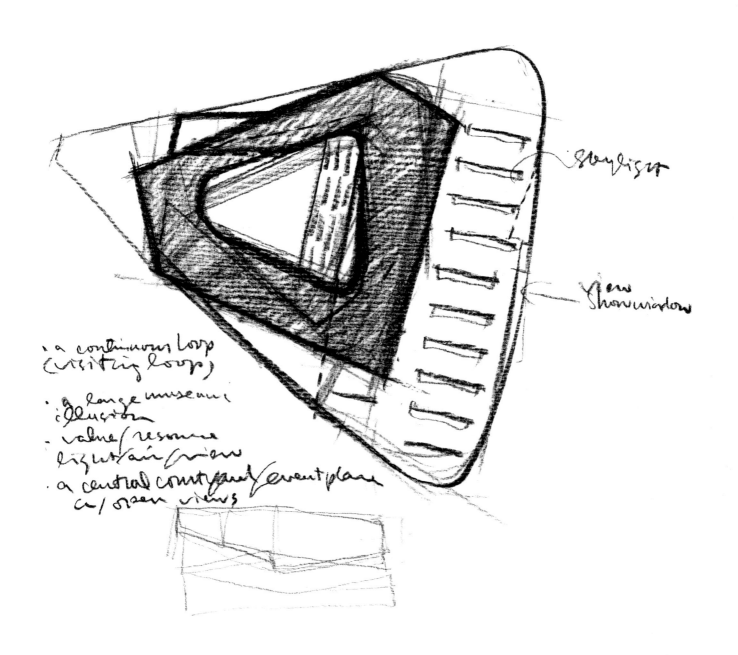

- a continuous loop
  (visiting loop)

- a large museum
  collection
- value/resource
  light/air/view
- a central courtyard/event place
  w/ open views

skylight

view
Showwindow

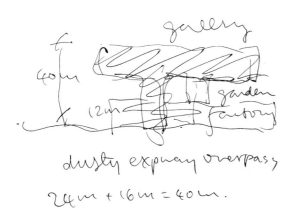

gallery

40m

12m

garden
factory

dusty expway overpass

24m + 16m = 40m.

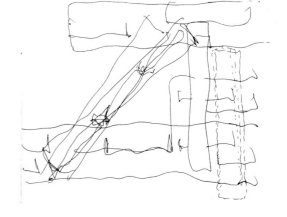

garden Artron Center

a loop?

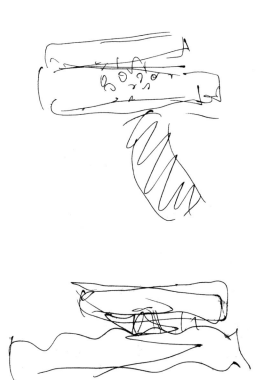

Artron
Center

Atr

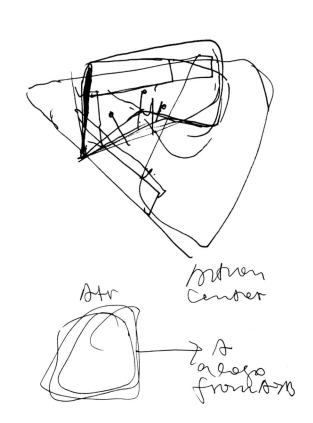

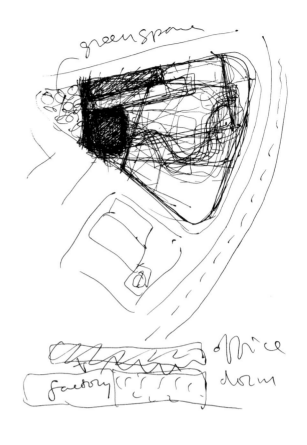

green space

office
dorm

factory

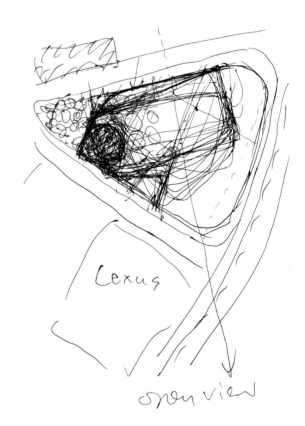

Lexus

open view

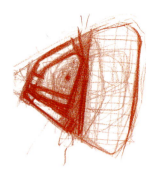

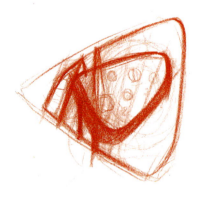
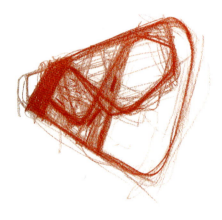

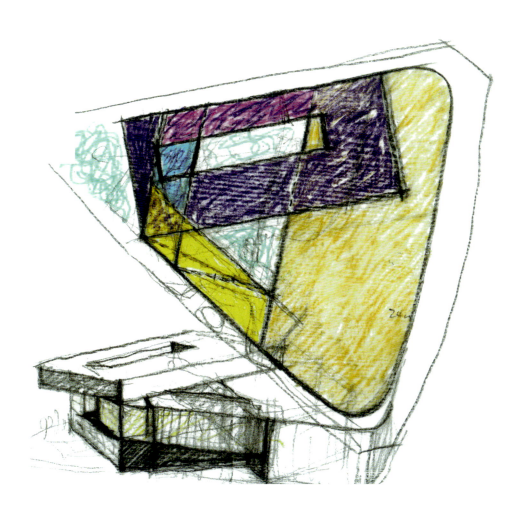

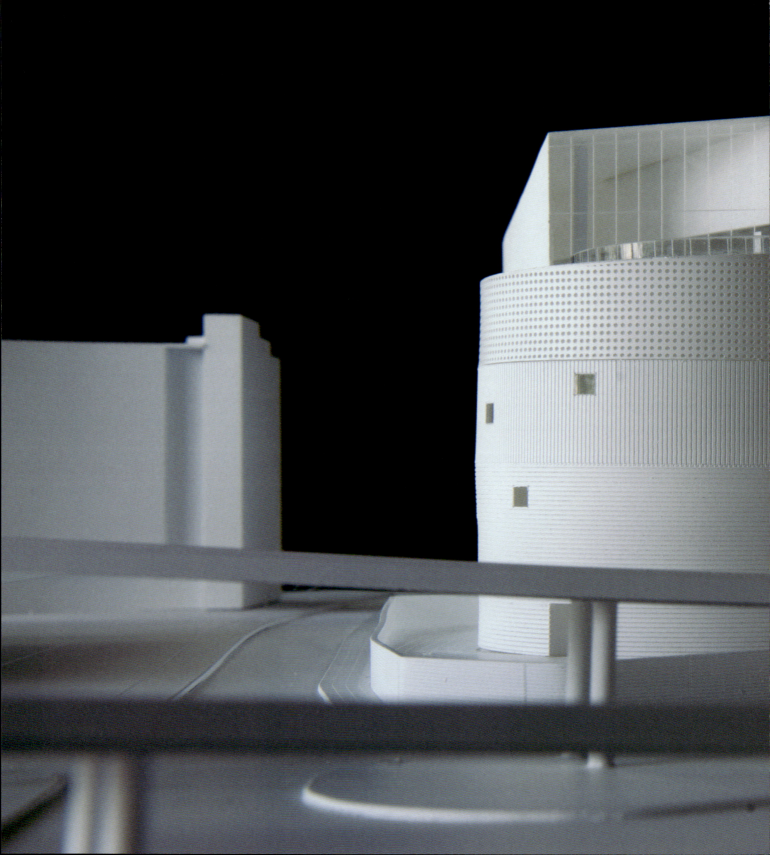

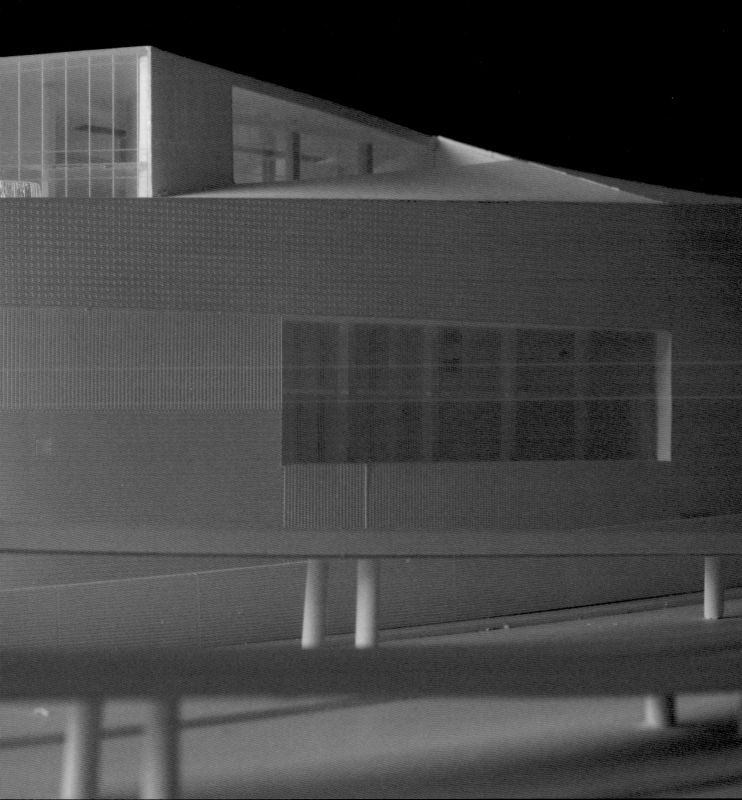

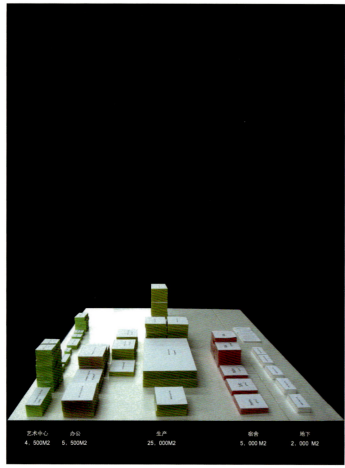

艺术中心　　办公　　　　　　　生产　　　　　　宿舍　　　地下
4,500M2　5,500M2　　　　　　25,000M2　　　　5,000 M2　2,000 M2

 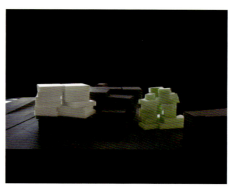 

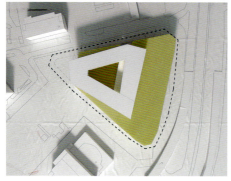 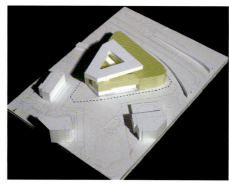 

  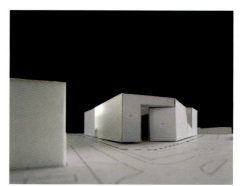

  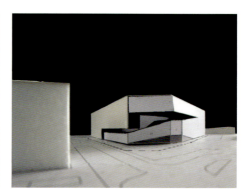

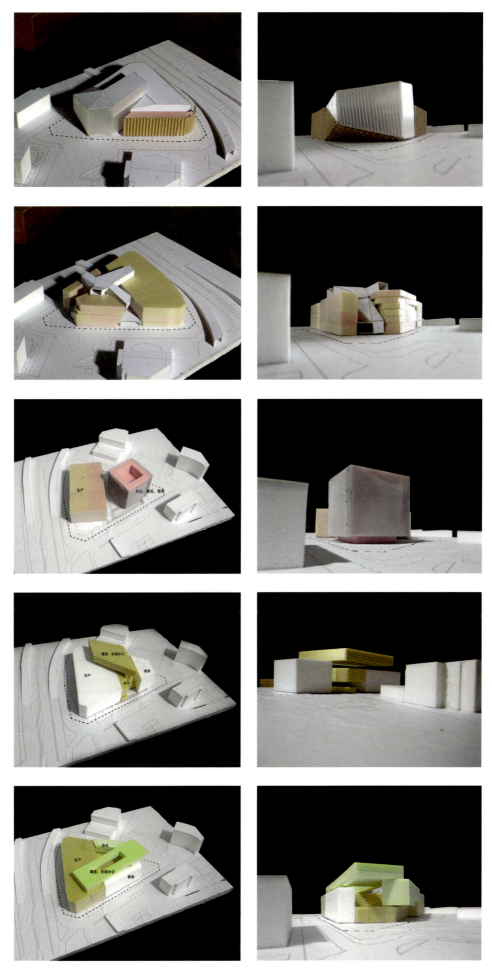

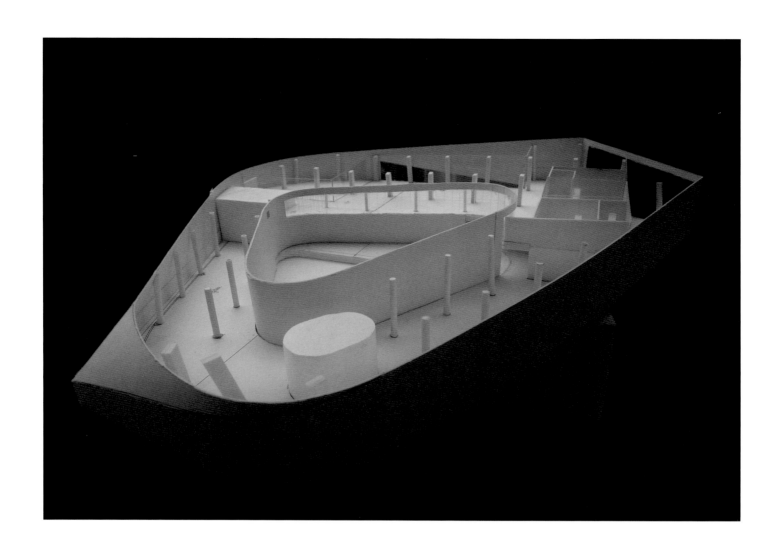

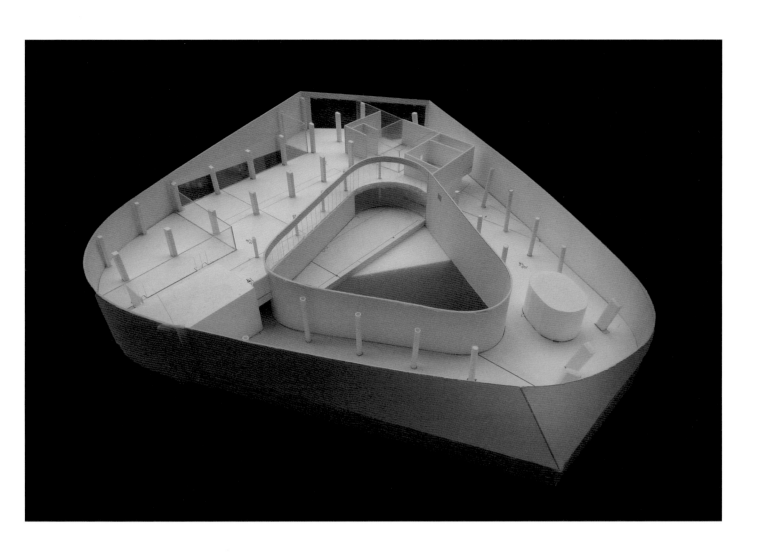

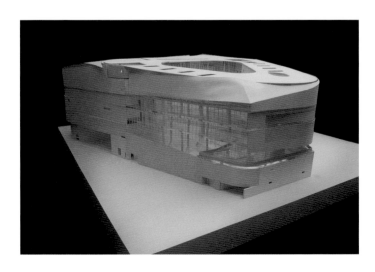

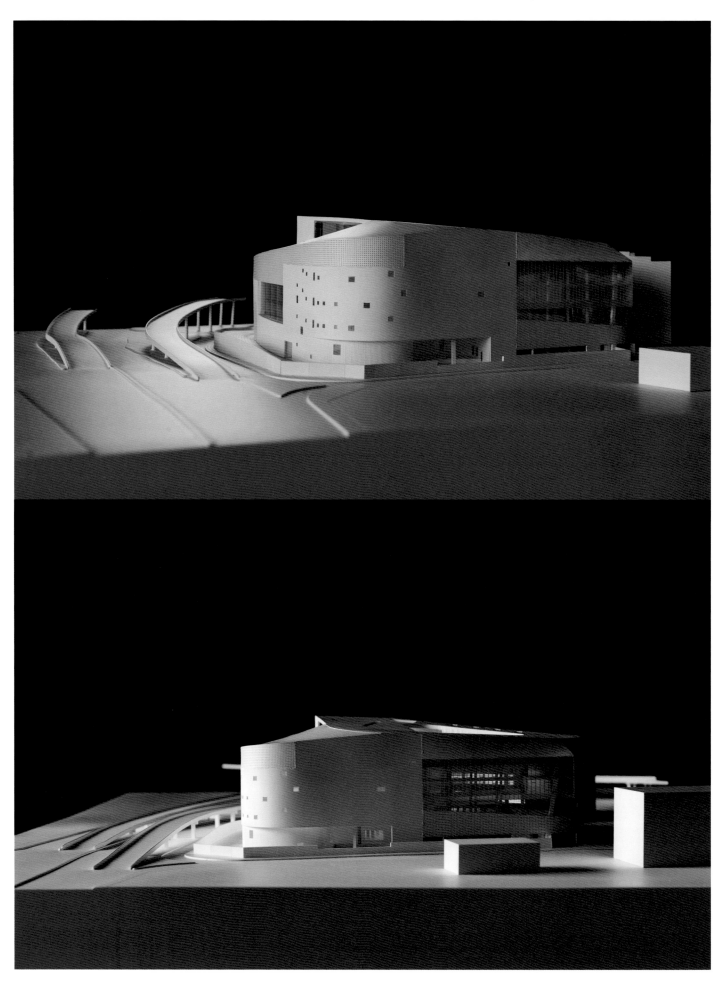

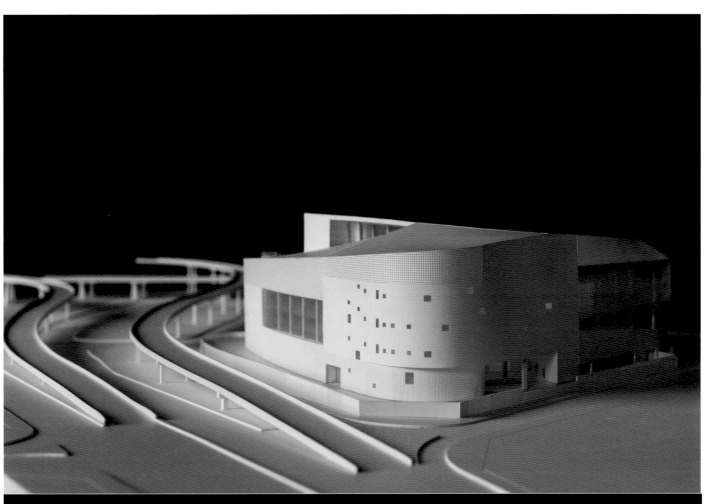

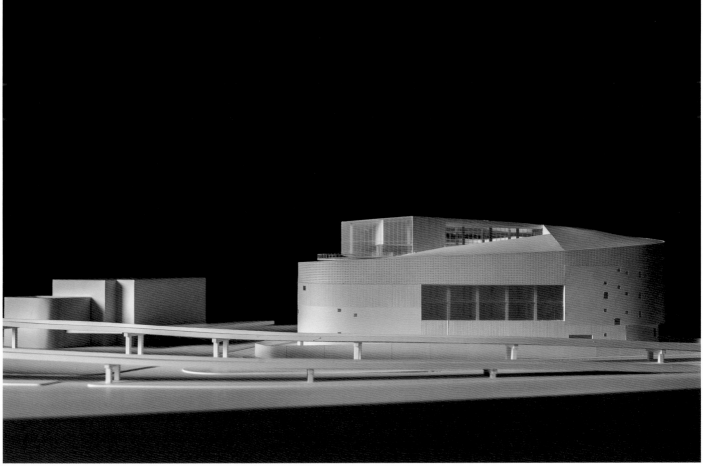

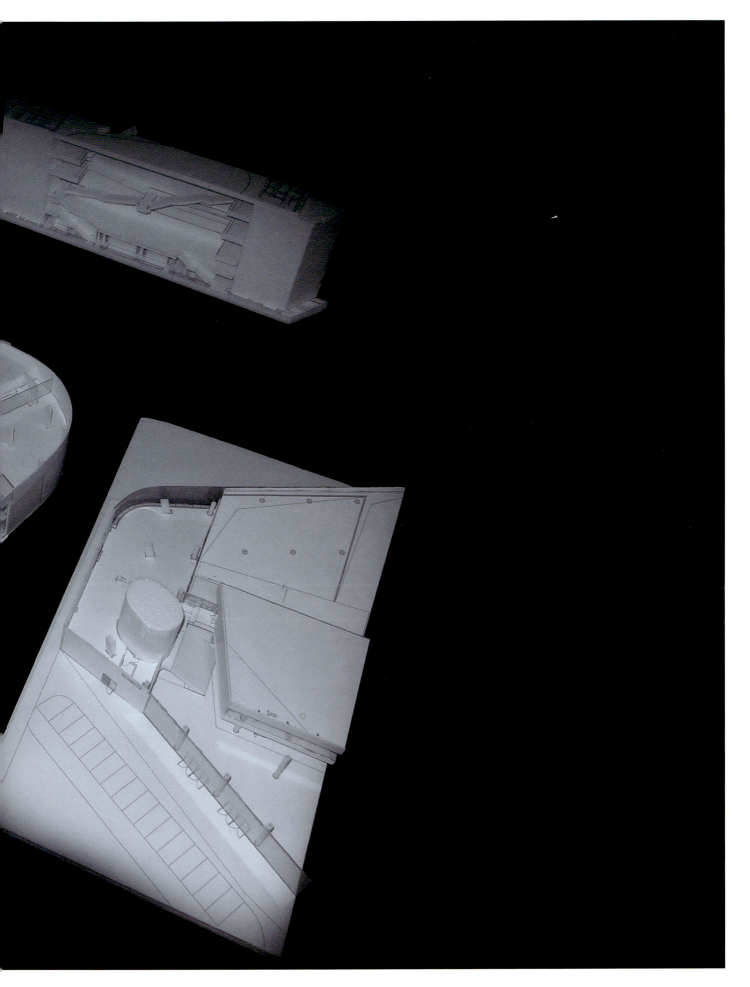

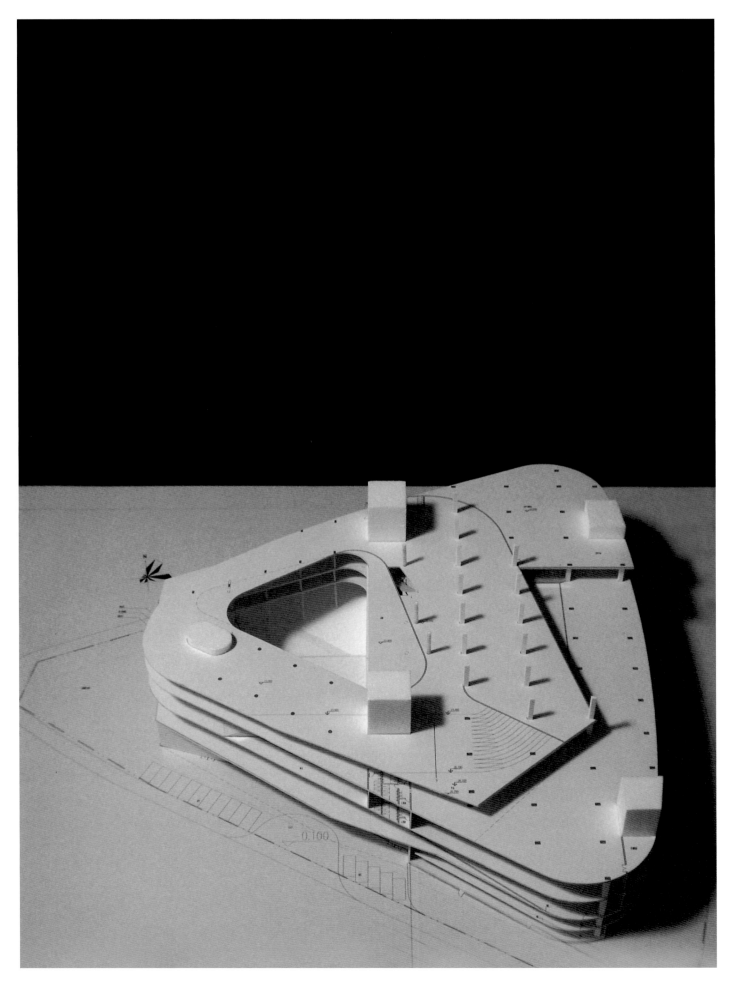

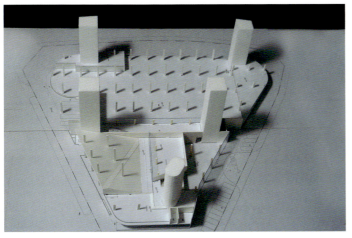
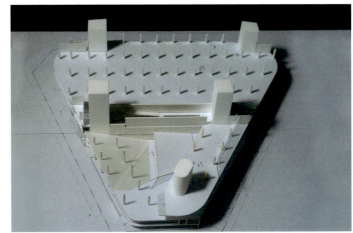
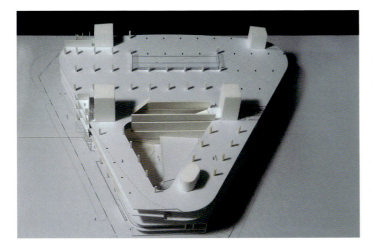
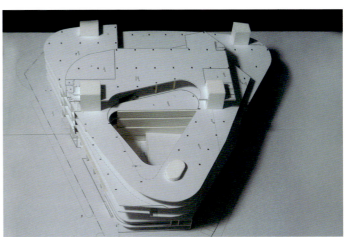
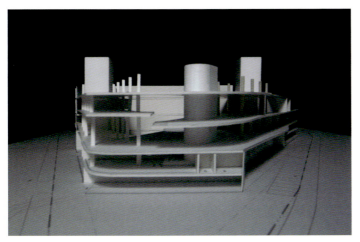
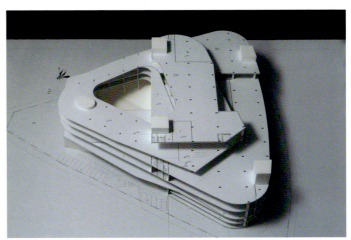

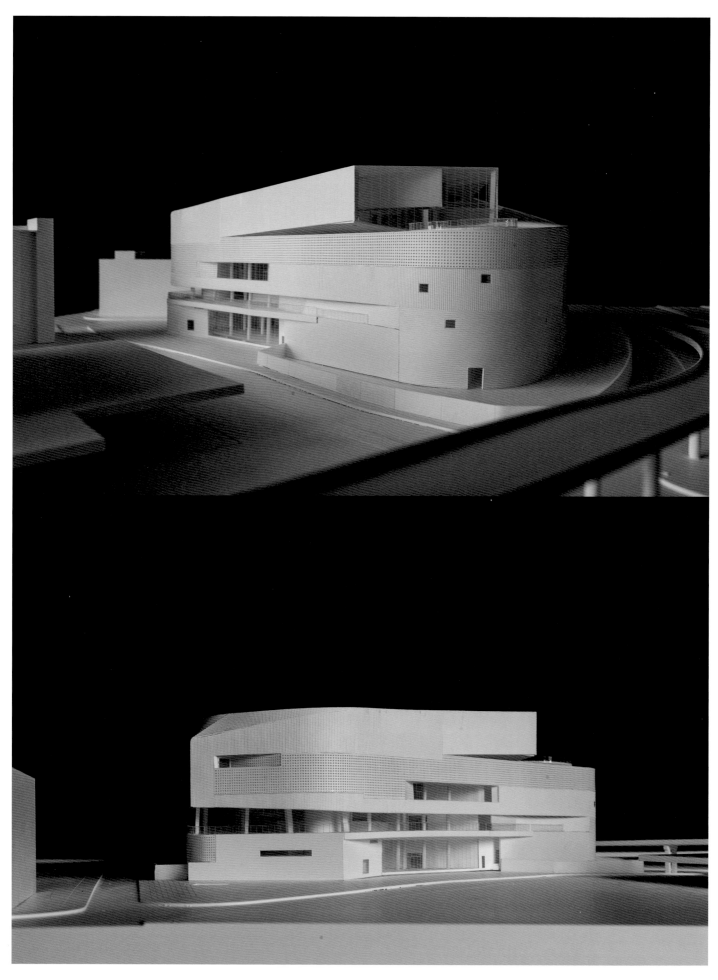

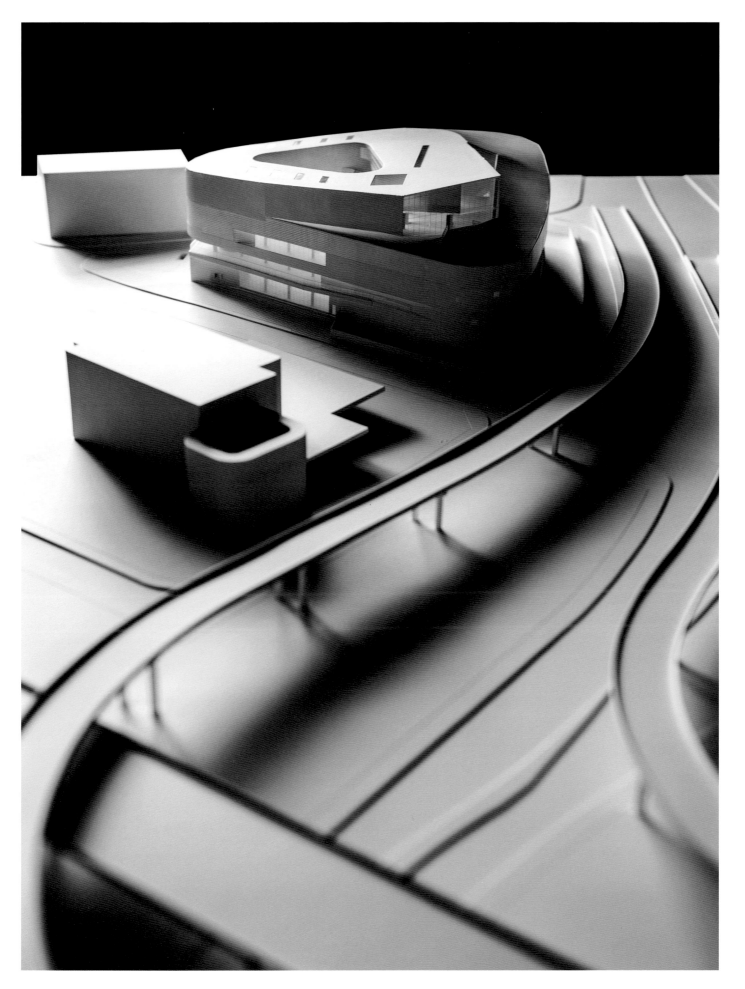

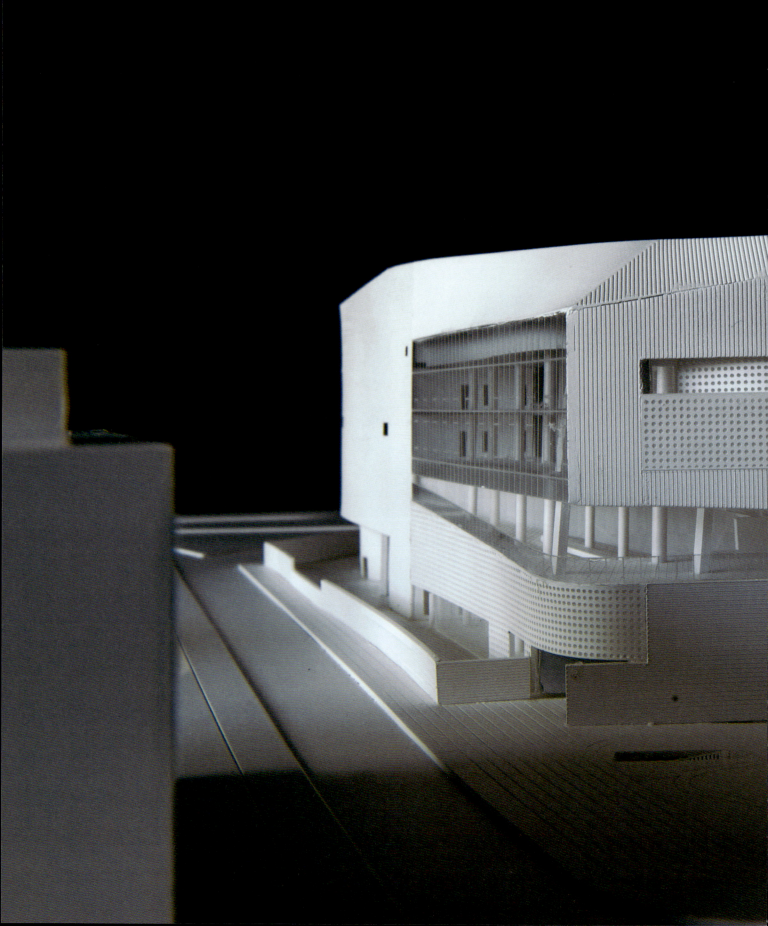

PRESENTATION DRAWINGS

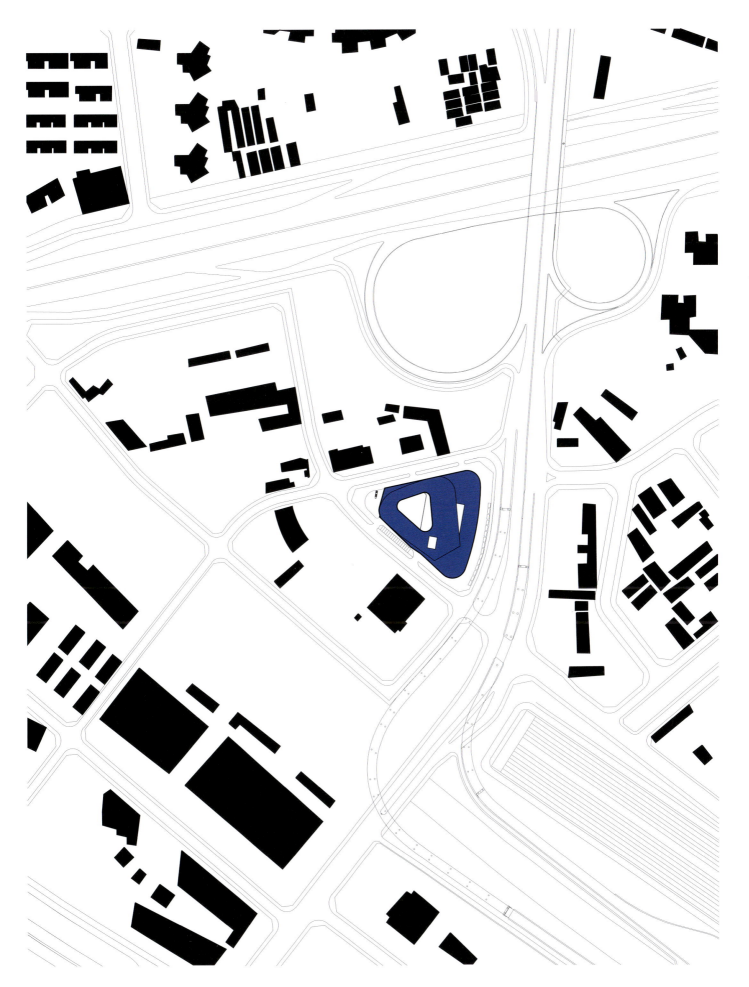

1 Gallery	16 Terrace
2 Canteen	17 Sloped Terrace
3 Library	18 Atrium
4 Office	19 Finished Product Storage
5 Printing Room	20 Manual Bcobinding
6 Loading Dock	21 Balcony
7 Ramp for Parking	22 Plate-Making
8 Main Entrance	23 Courtyard
9 Air Conditioning	24 Exterior Terrace
10 Break Room	25 Gallery Exhibition
11 Multifunctional Hall	26 Art Archive Storage
12 Atrium Archive	27 Design Studio
13 Void above Printing Room	28 Mechanical Equipment
14 Coffee & Book Shop	29 Auction Catalogue Archive
15 Mechanical Bookbinding	30 Office of the Chairman

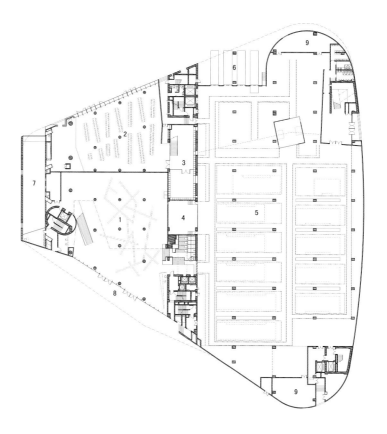

0 2   6   12m

First Floor Plan

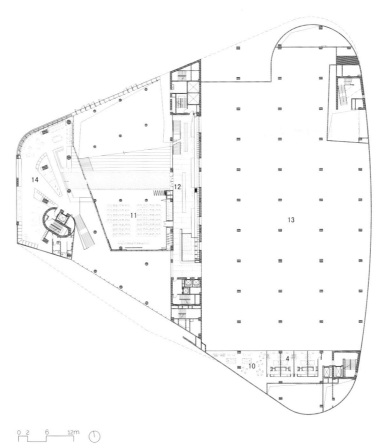

0 2 6 12m

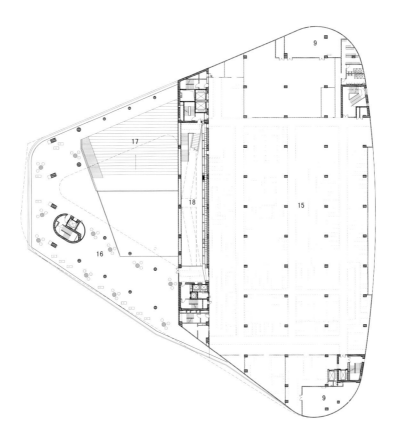

0 2 6 12m

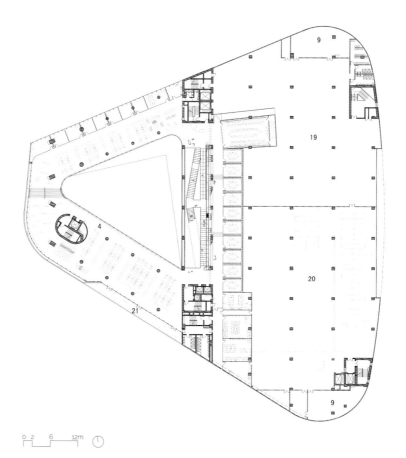

0 2   6   12m

Third Floor Plan

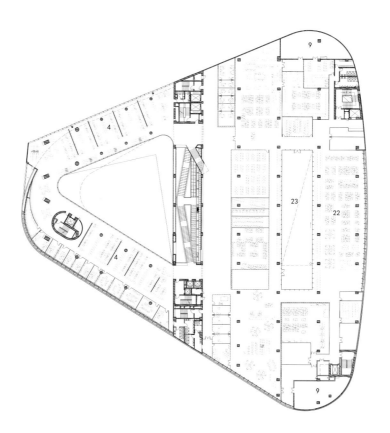

0 2   6   12m

Fourth Floor Plan

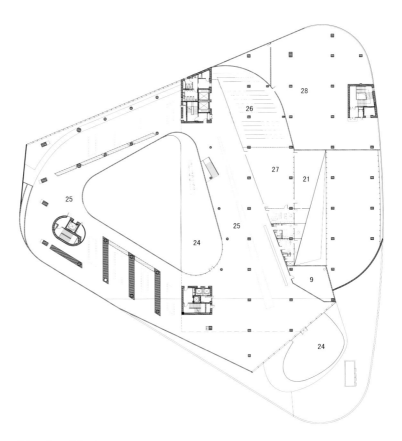

Fifth Floor Plan

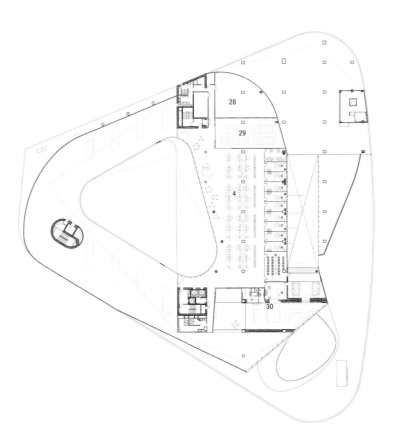

Sixth Floor Plan

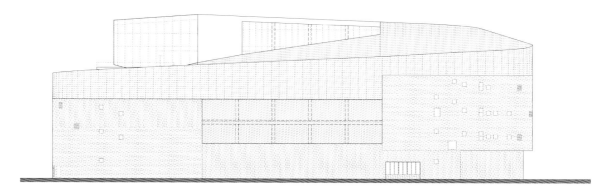

East Elevation

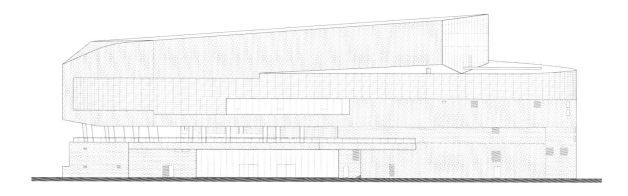

South Elevation

0   4   12   24m

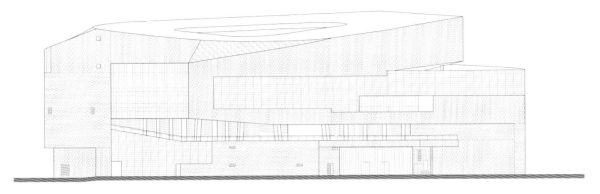

West Elevation

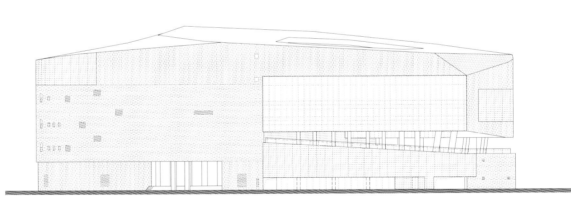

North Elevation

0   4   12   24m

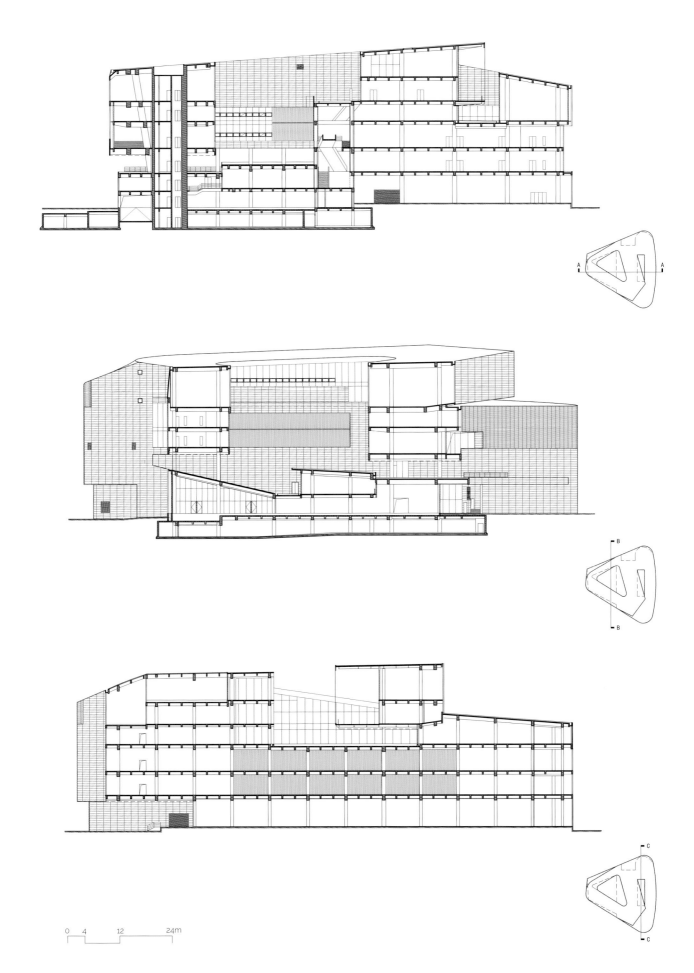

A   A

B

B

C

C

0   4   12   24m

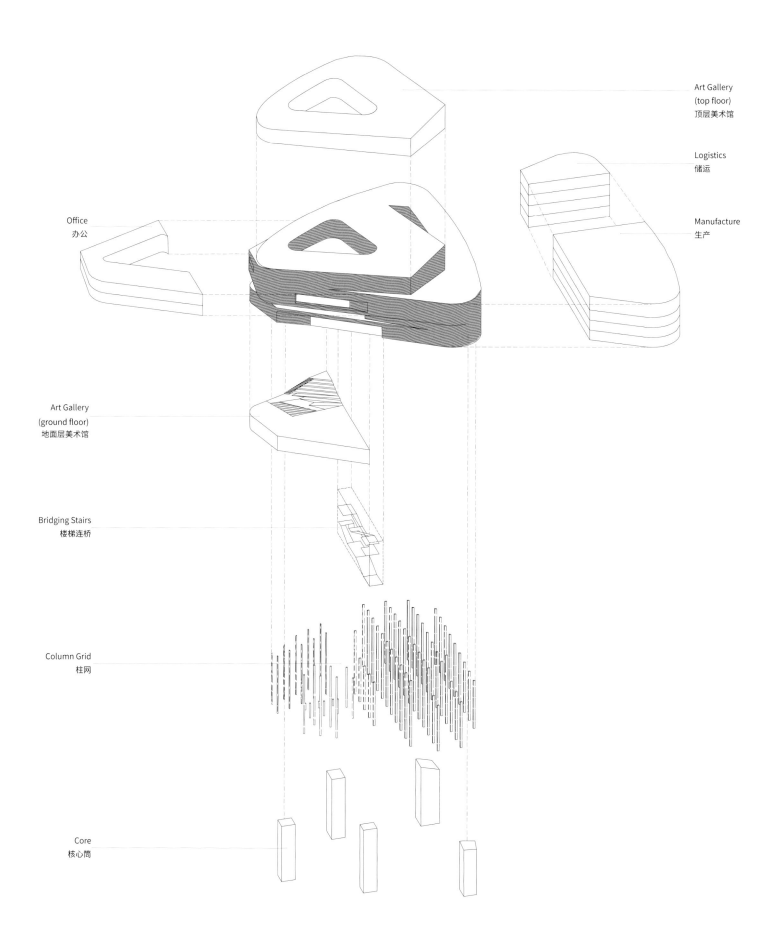

Art Gallery
(top floor)
顶层美术馆

Logistics
储运

Office
办公

Manufacture
生产

Art Gallery
(ground floor)
地面层美术馆

Bridging Stairs
楼梯连桥

Column Grid
柱网

Core
核心筒

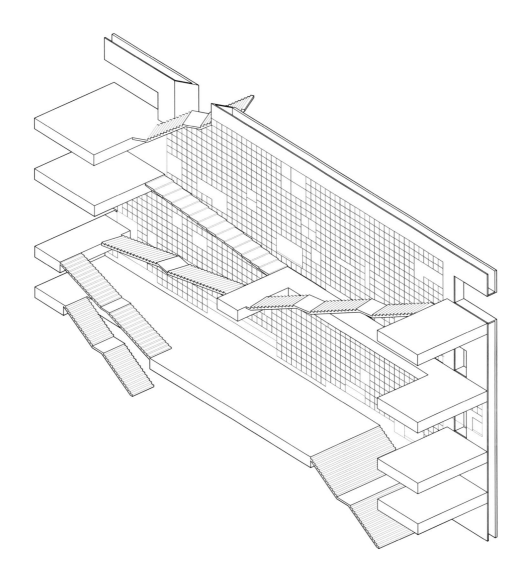

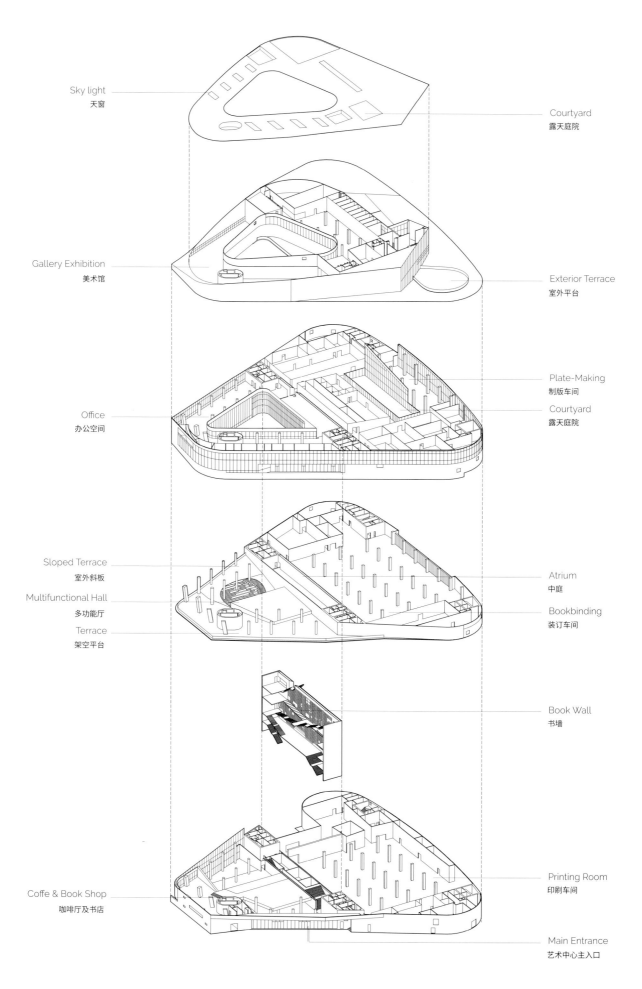

Sky light
天窗

Courtyard
露天庭院

Gallery Exhibition
美术馆

Exterior Terrace
室外平台

Plate-Making
制版车间

Office
办公空间

Courtyard
露天庭院

Sloped Terrace
室外斜板

Atrium
中庭

Multifunctional Hall
多功能厅

Bookbinding
装订车间

Terrace
架空平台

Book Wall
书墙

Printing Room
印刷车间

Coffe & Book Shop
咖啡厅及书店

Main Entrance
艺术中心主入口

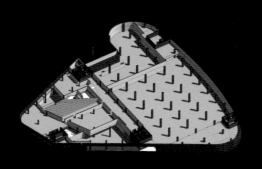
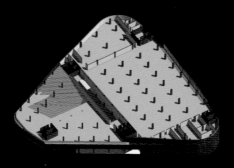
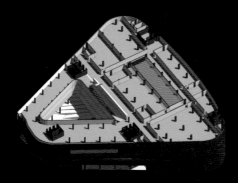
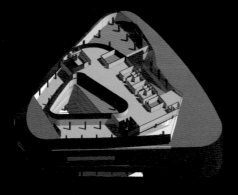
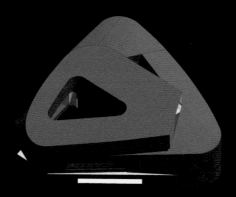

RENDERINGS

Renderings on this spread by Wendell Burnette Architects

CONSTRUCTION

WORKING DRAWINGS

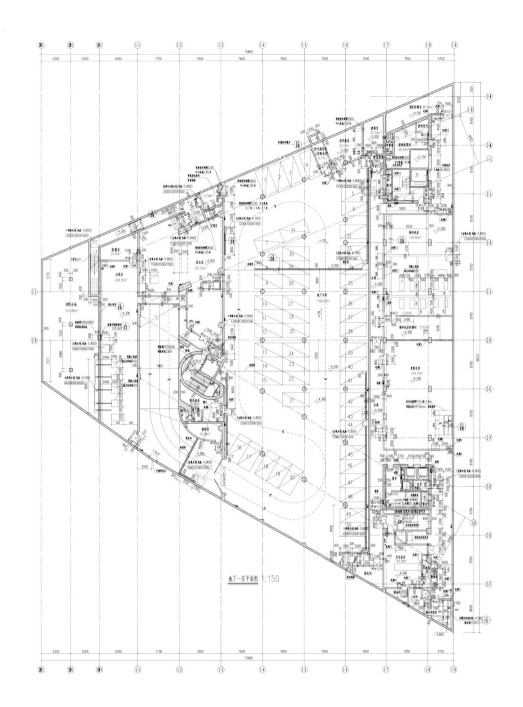

地下一层平面图 1:150

Basement Floor Plan

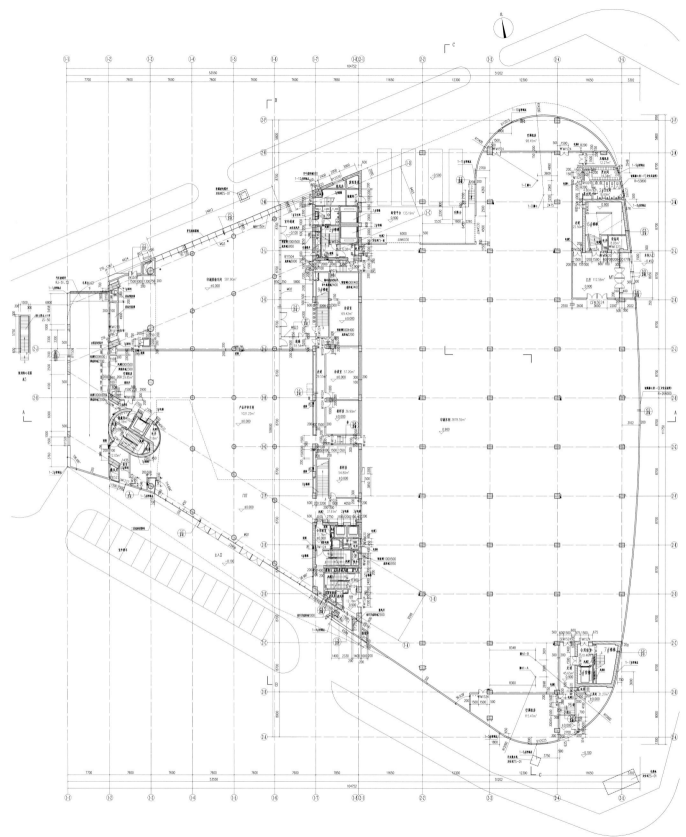

First Floor Plan

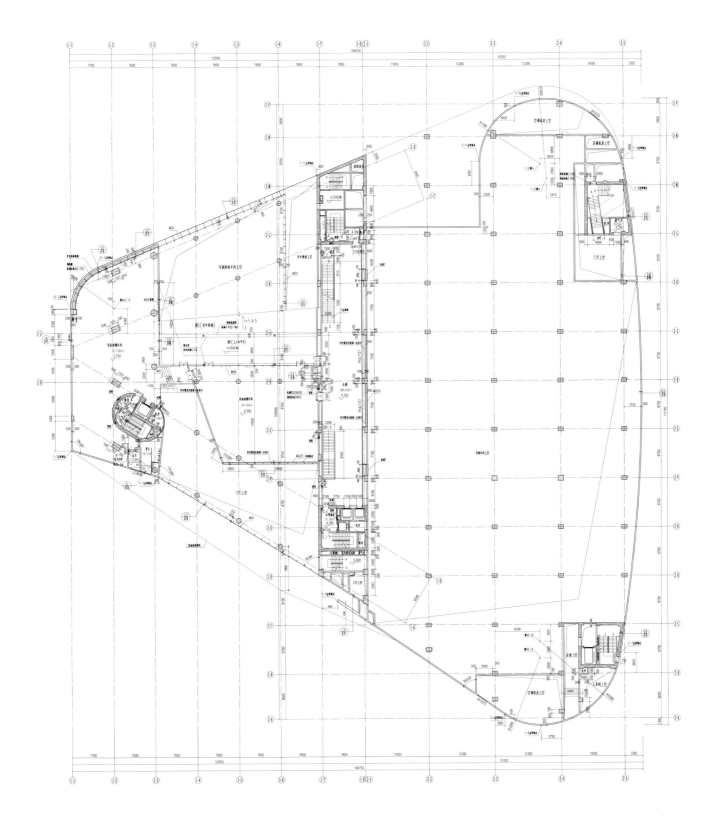

Mezzanine Floor Plan

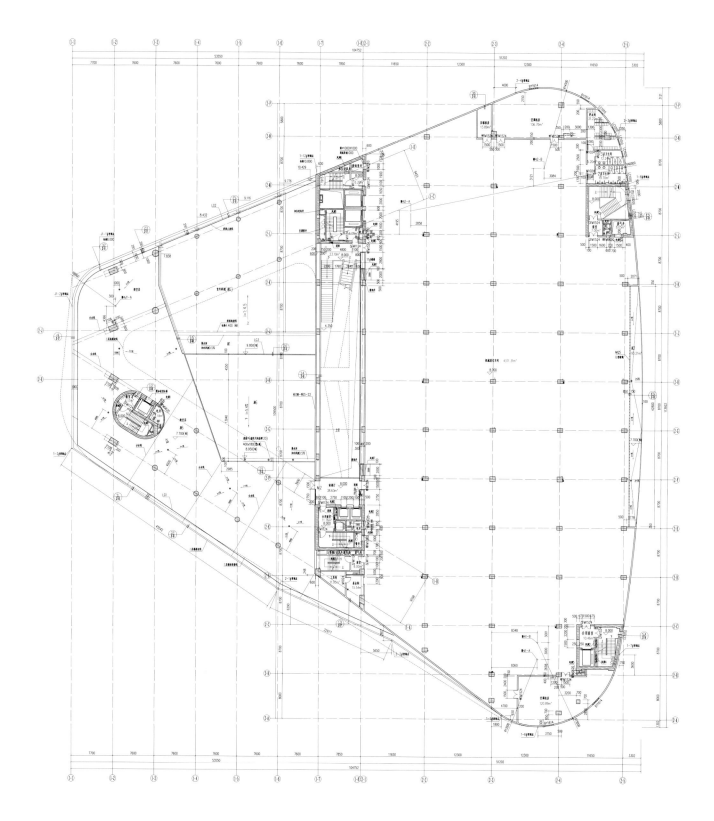

Second Floor Plan

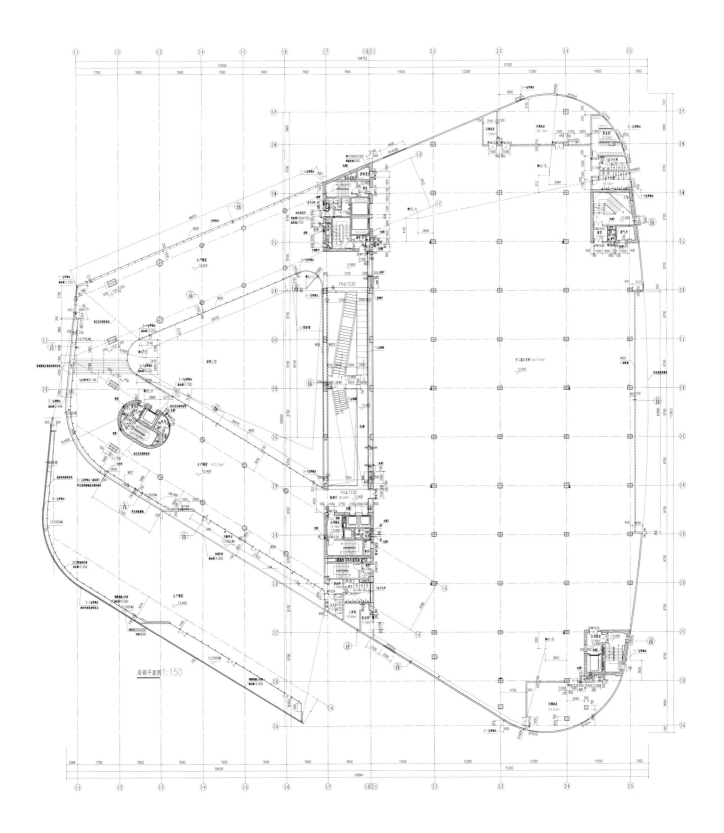

局部平面图1:150

Third Floor Plan

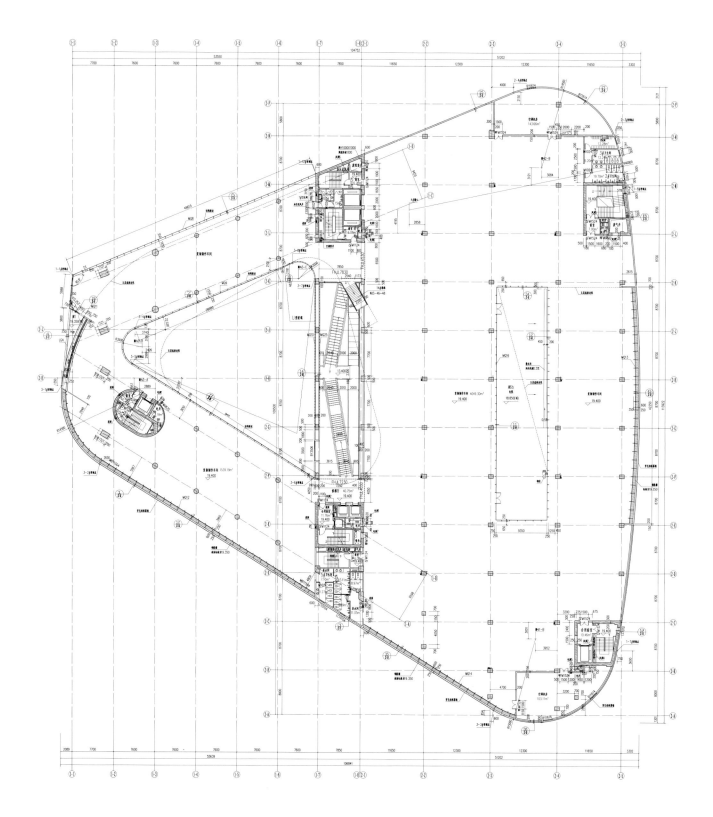

Fourth Floor Plan

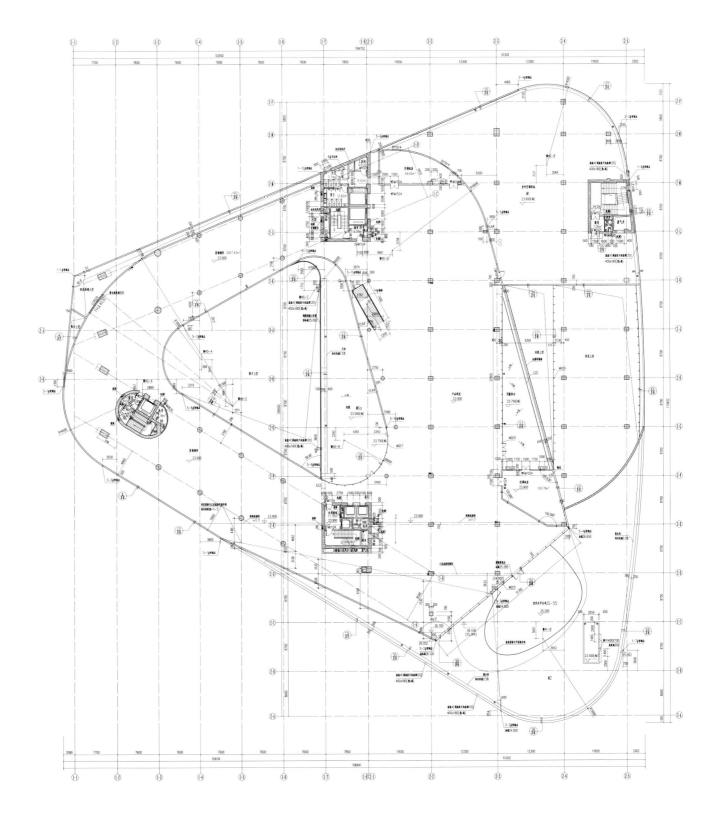

Fifth Floor Plan

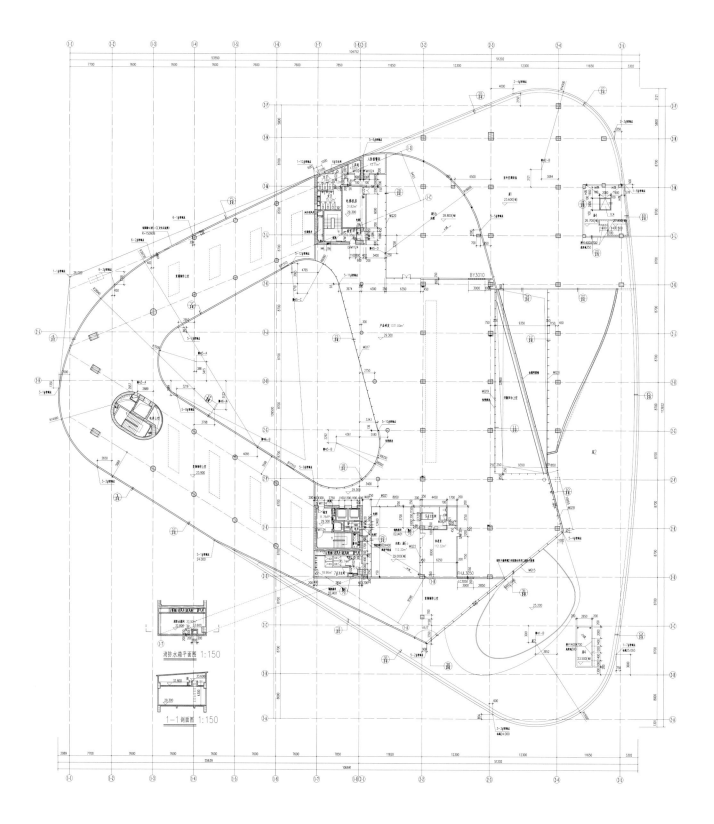

消防水箱平面图 1:150

1—1剖面图 1:150

Sixth Floor Plan

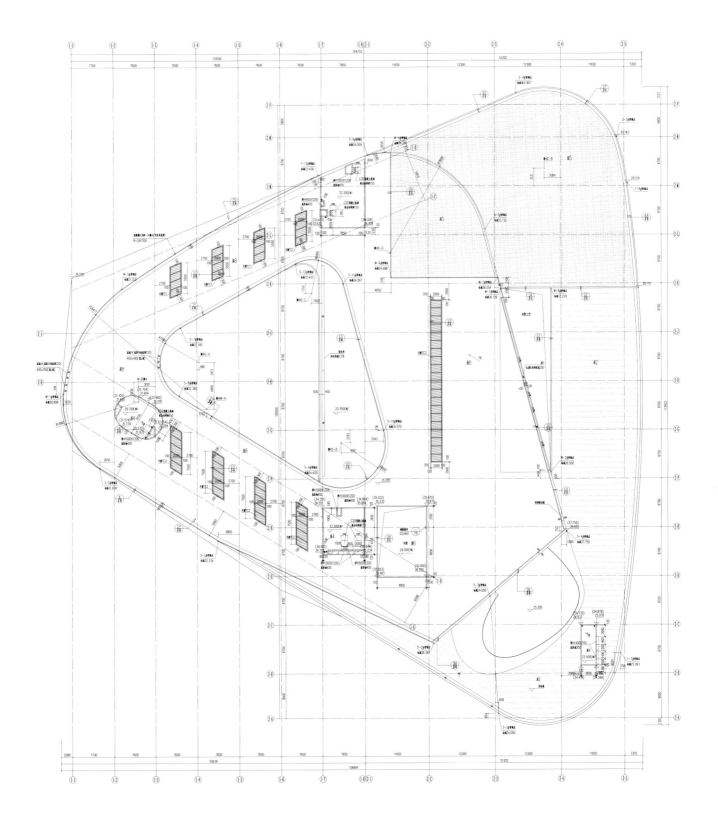

Roof Plan

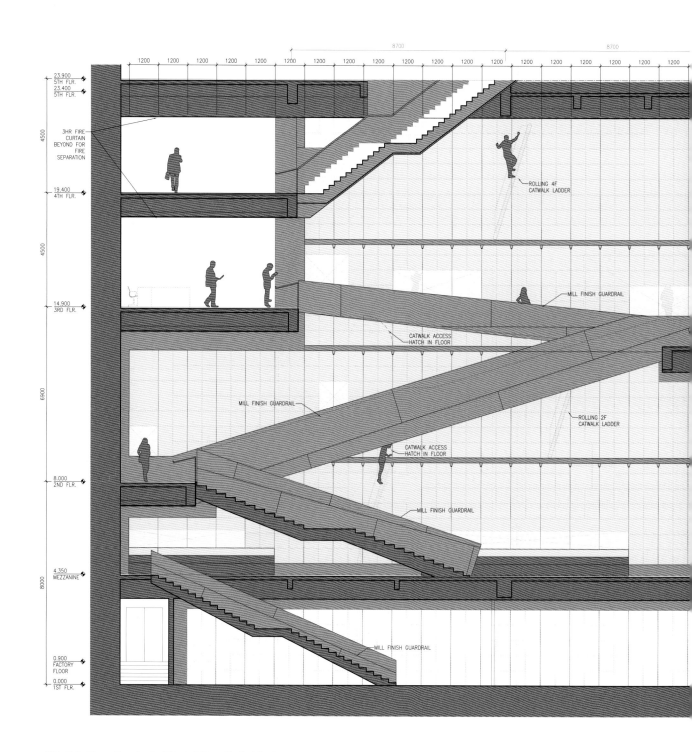

Atrium Archive - Drawing by Wendell Burnette Architects

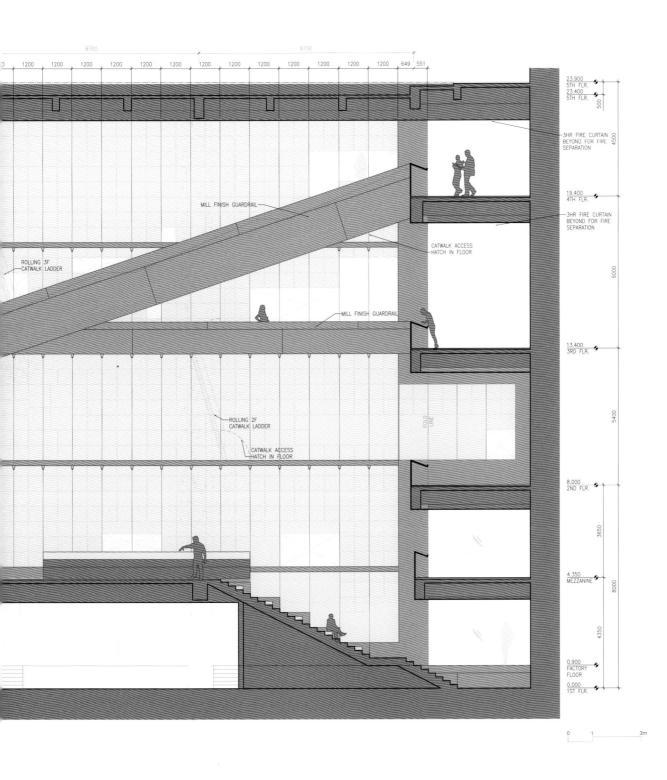

8700
8700

1200 | 1200 | 1200 | 1200 | 1200 | 1200 | 1200 | 1200 | 1200 | 1200 | 1200 | 649 | 551

23.900
5TH FLR.
23.400
5TH FLR.

500

3HR FIRE CURTAIN
BEYOND FOR FIRE
SEPARATION

4500

MILL FINISH GUARDRAIL

19.400
4TH FLR.

3HR FIRE CURTAIN
BEYOND FOR FIRE
SEPARATION

CATWALK ACCESS
HATCH IN FLOOR

6000

ROLLING 3F
CATWALK LADDER

MILL FINISH GUARDRAIL

13.400
3RD FLR.

ROLLING 2F
CATWALK LADDER

FOLD
LINE

5400

CATWALK ACCESS
HATCH IN FLOOR

8.000
2ND FLR.

3650

4.350
MEZZANINE

8000

4350

0.900
FACTORY
FLOOR
0.000
1ST FLR.

0   1   3m

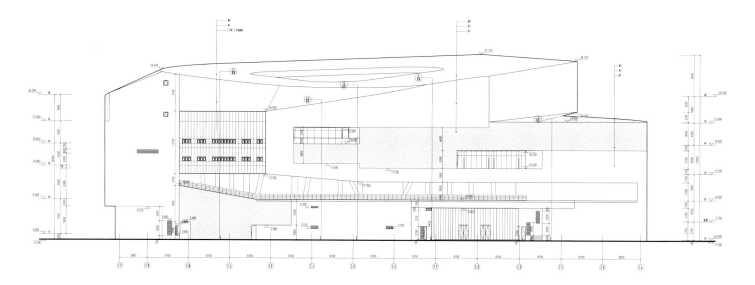

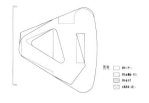

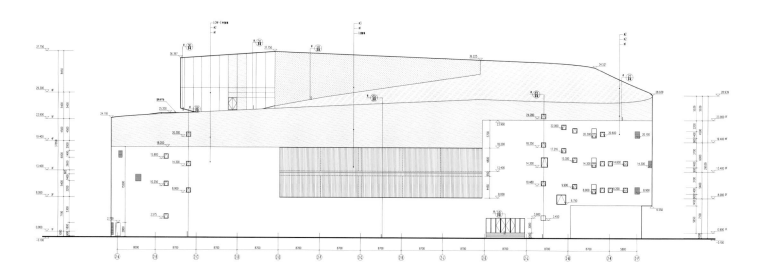

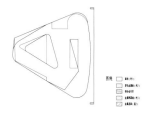

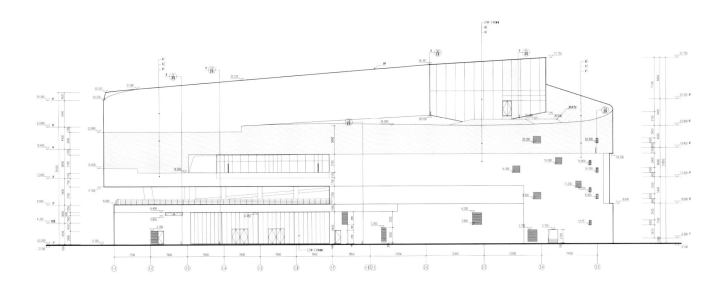

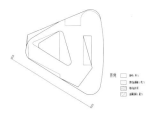

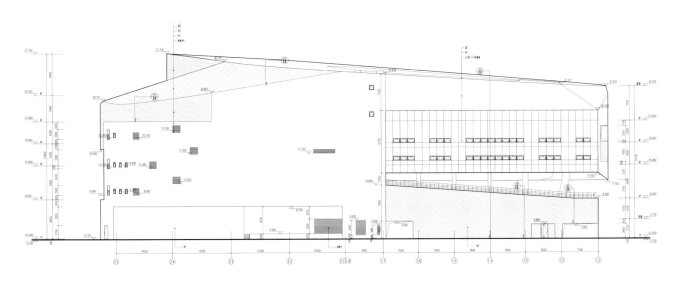

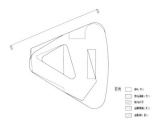

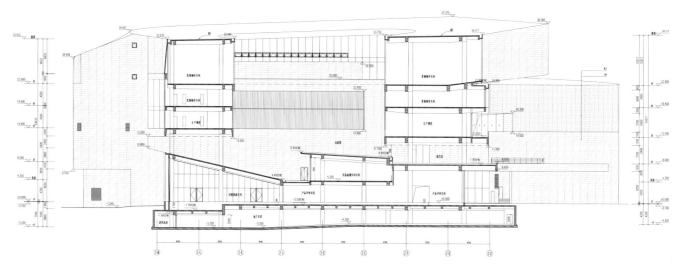

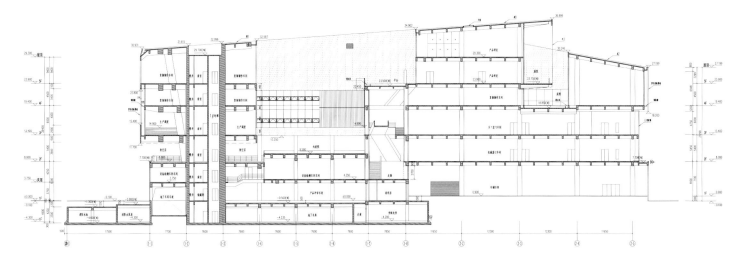

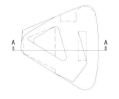

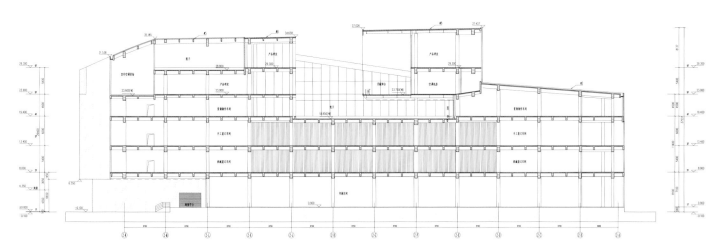

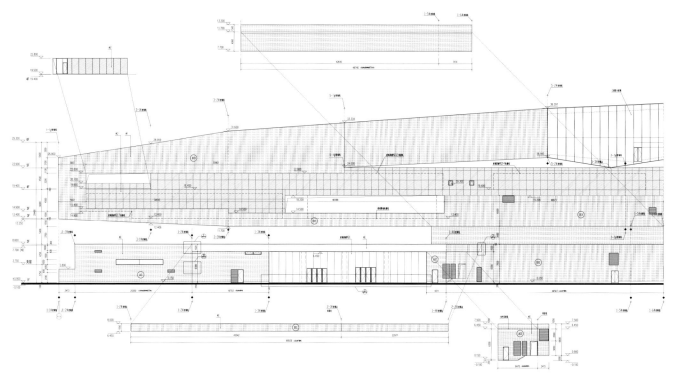

Southwest Expanded Elevation of Wall Tiles

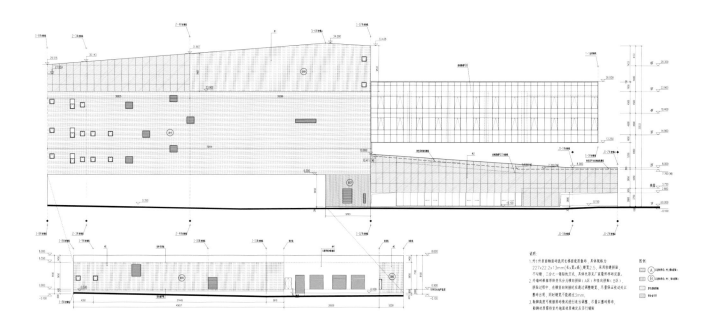

Northwest Expanded Elevation of Wall Tiles

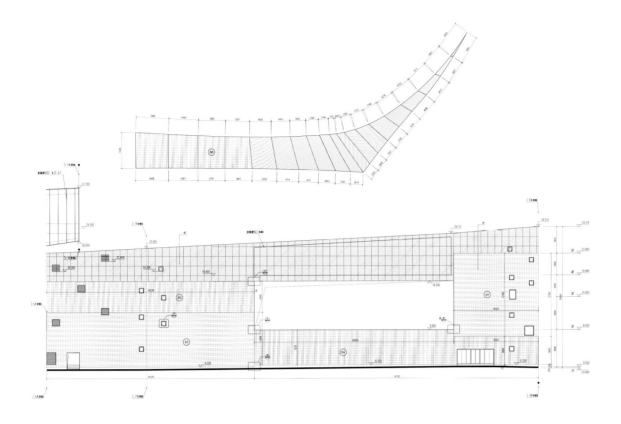

East Expanded Elevation of Wall Tiles

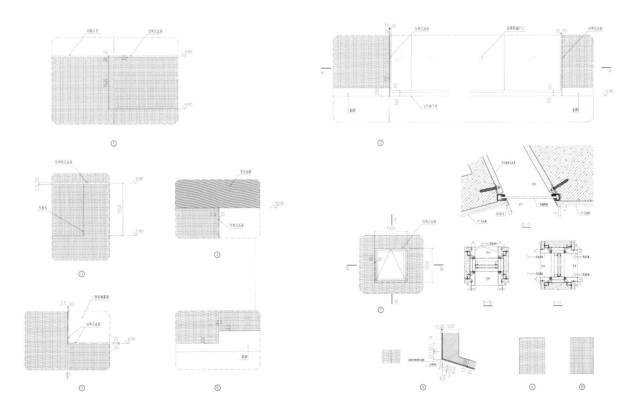

Details of Wall Tiles

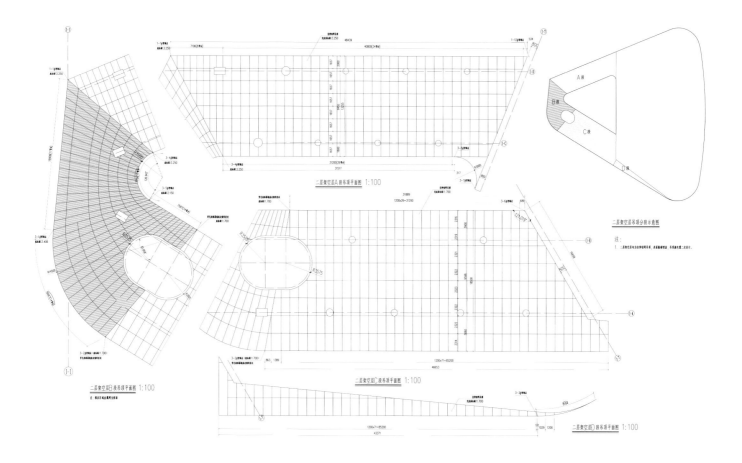

2F Exterior Suspended Ceiling

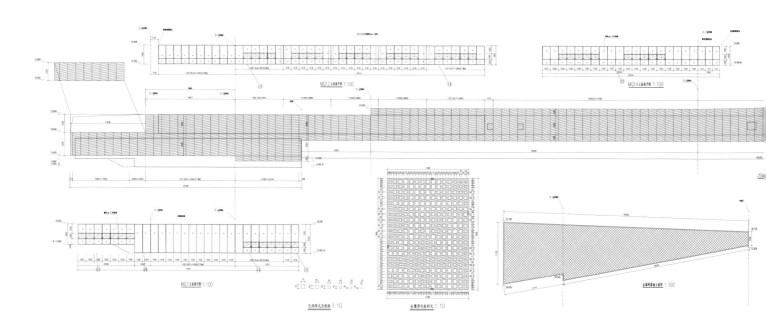

Curtain Wall Expanded View

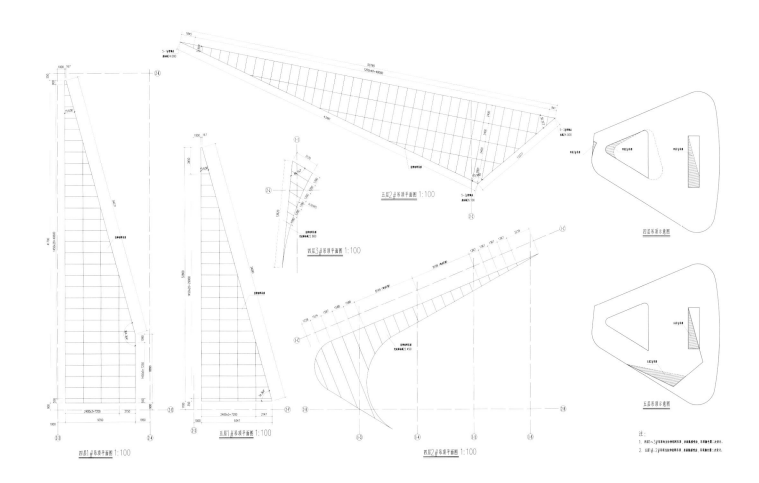

五层2#吊顶平面图 1:100

四层3#吊顶平面图 1:100

四层1#吊顶平面图 1:100

五层1#吊顶平面图 1:100

四层2#吊顶平面图 1:100

四层吊顶示意图

五层吊顶示意图

注：
1. 四层1~3#吊顶为拉伸钢网吊顶，表面氟碳喷涂，另见建筑工程二次设计。
2. 五层1#吊顶为拉伸钢网吊顶，表面氟碳喷涂，另见建筑工程二次设计。

4F & 5F Exterior Suspended Ceiling

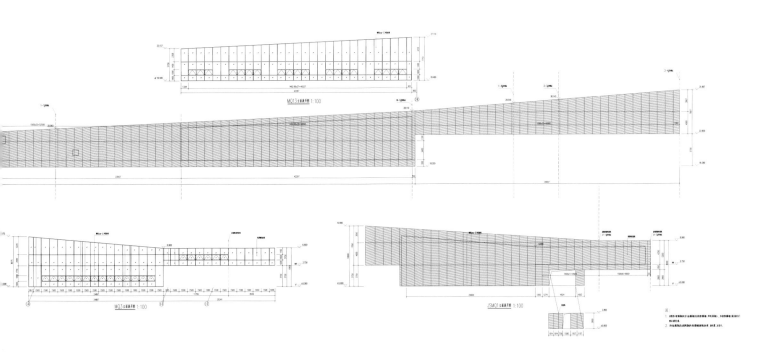

MQ13立面展开图 1:100

MQ3立面展开图 1:100

JSMQ1立面展开图 1:100

105

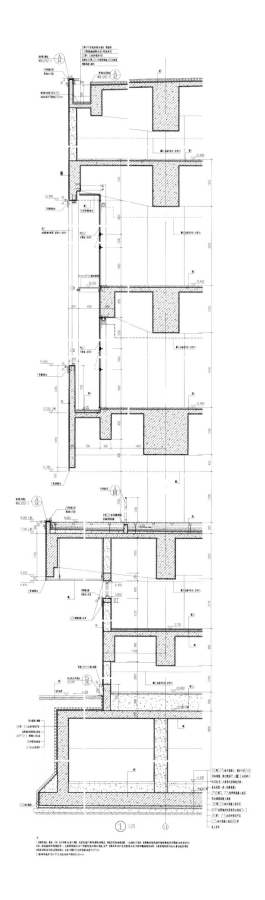

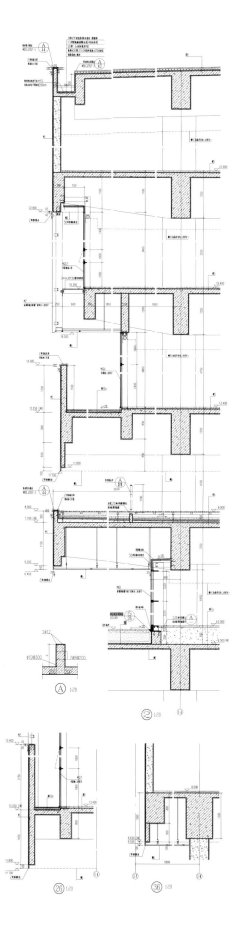

Wall Section

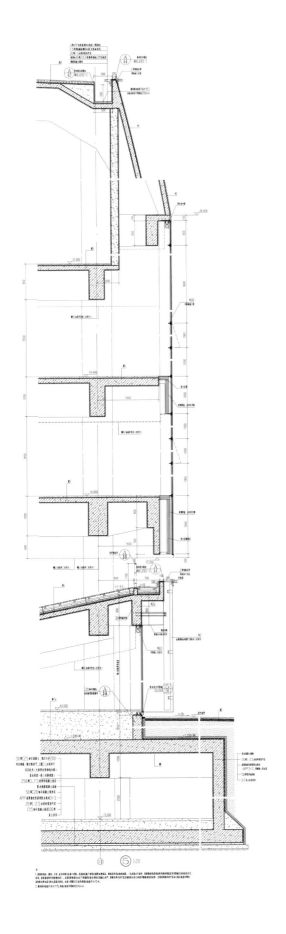

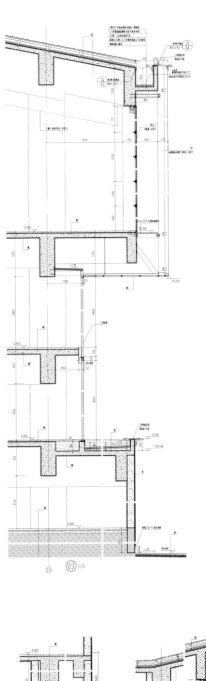

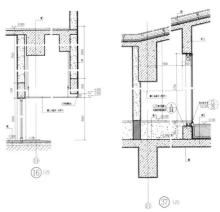

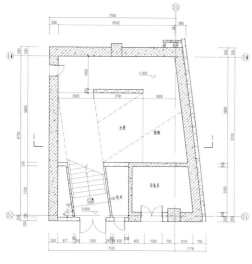

6#楼梯一层平面图 1:50

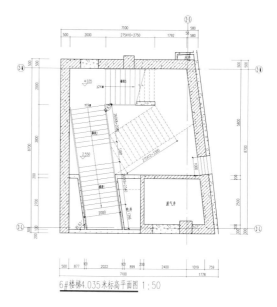

6#楼梯4.035米标高平面图 1:50

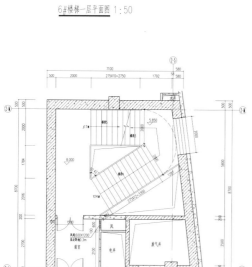

6#楼梯二层平面图 1:50

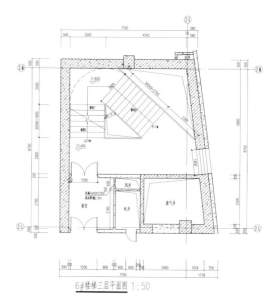

6#楼梯三层平面图 1:50

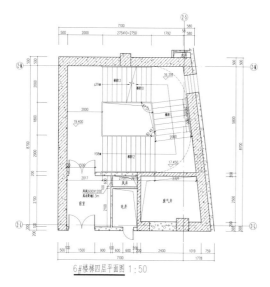

6#楼梯四层平面图 1:50

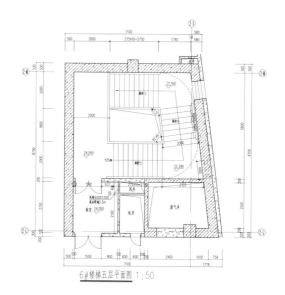

6#楼梯五层平面图 1:50

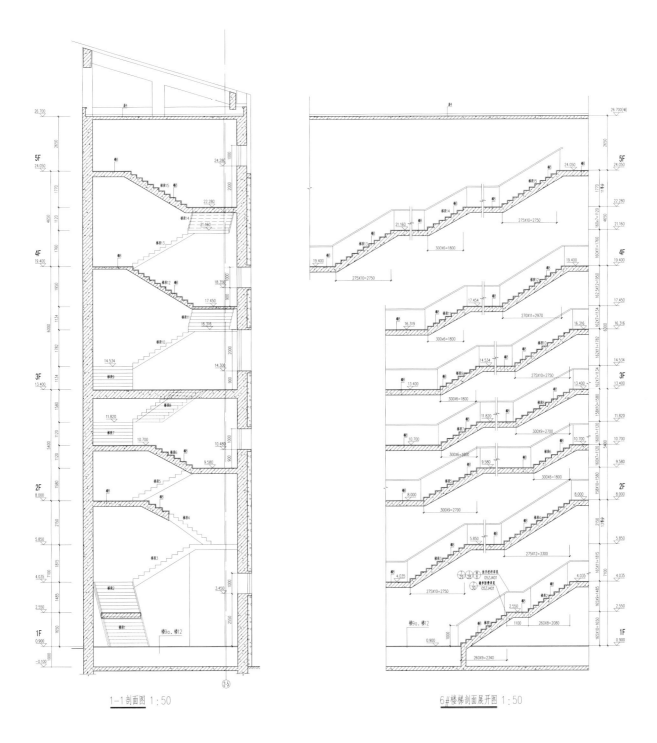

1-1剖面图 1:50

6#楼梯剖面展开图 1:50

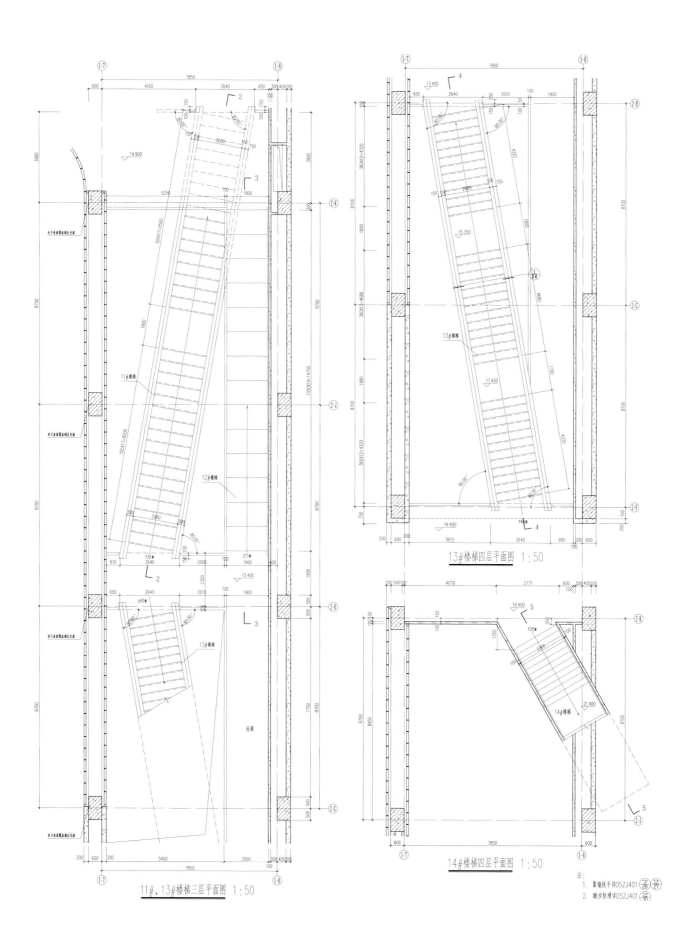

11#、13#楼梯三层平面图 1:50

13#楼梯四层平面图 1:50

14#楼梯四层平面图 1:50

注：
1. 靠墙扶手详05ZJ401 ⑳㉗
2. 踏步防滑详05ZJ401 ㉓

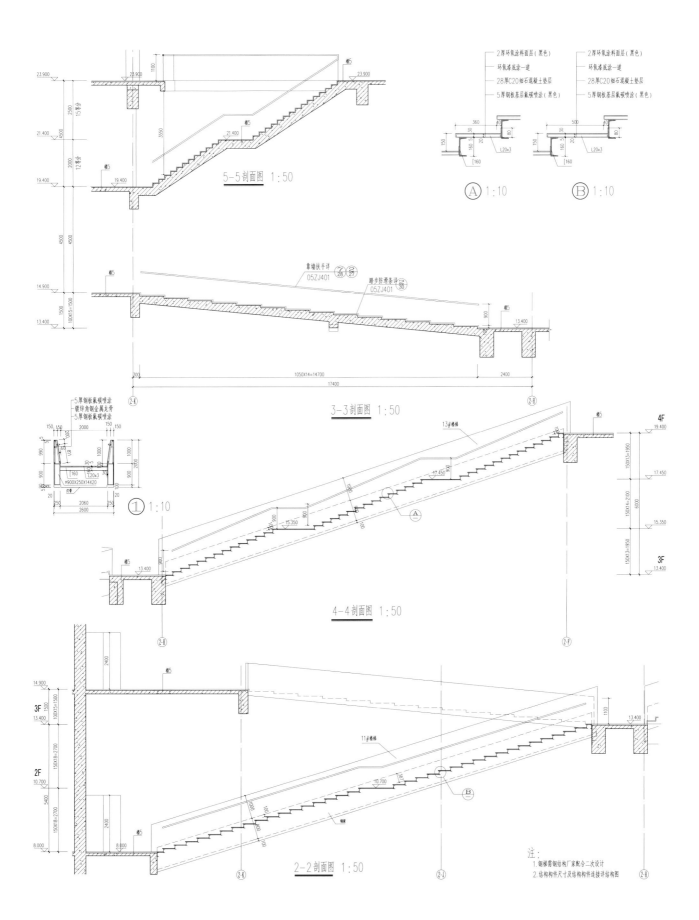

5-5 剖面图 1:50

2厚环氧涂料面层（黑色）
环氧漆底涂一遍
28厚C20细石混凝土垫层
5厚钢板基层氟碳喷涂（黑色）

2厚环氧涂料面层（黑色）
环氧漆底涂一遍
28厚C20细石混凝土垫层
5厚钢板基层氟碳喷涂（黑色）

Ⓐ 1:10   Ⓑ 1:10

矮墙扶手详 05ZJ401
踏步防滑条详 05ZJ401

3-3 剖面图 1:50

5厚钢板氟碳喷涂
镀锌角钢金属龙骨
5厚钢板氟碳喷涂

① 1:10

13#楼梯

4-4 剖面图 1:50

11#楼梯

2-2 剖面图 1:50

注:
1. 钢梯需钢结构厂家配合二次设计
2. 结构构件尺寸及结构构件连接详结构图

PROCESS

113

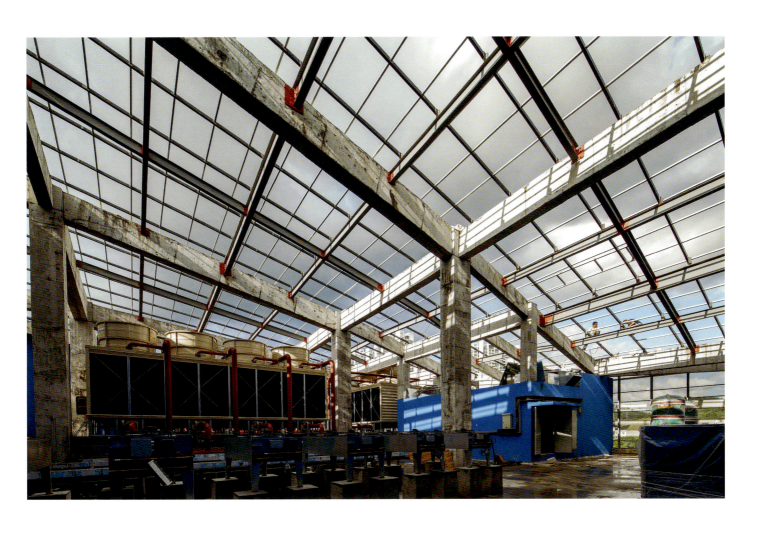

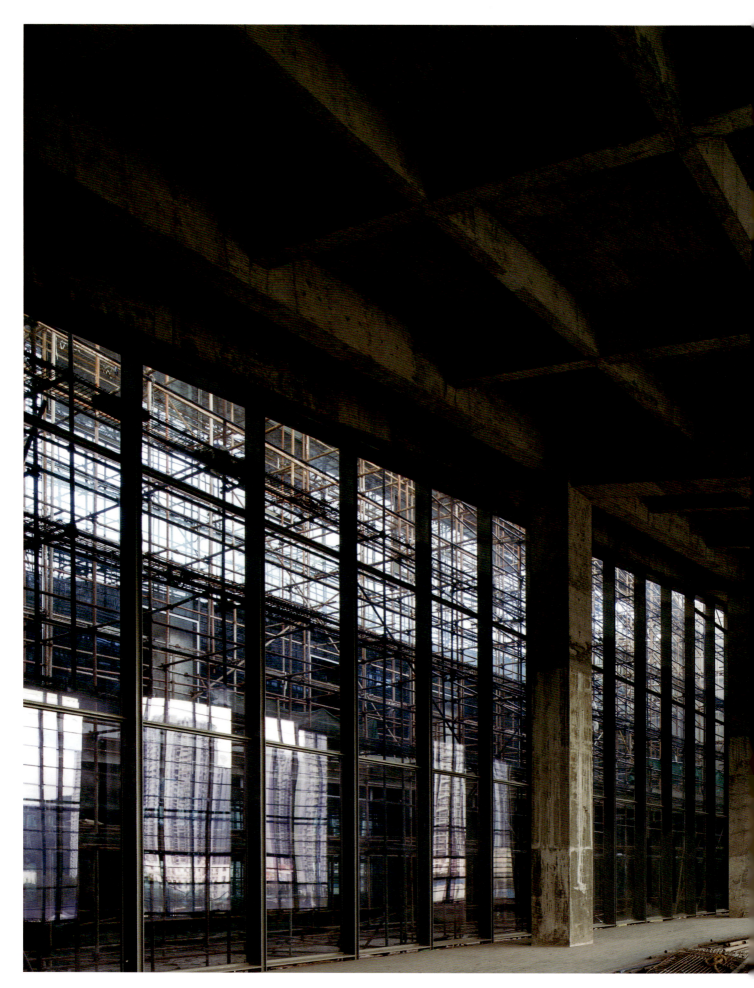

THE BUILDING

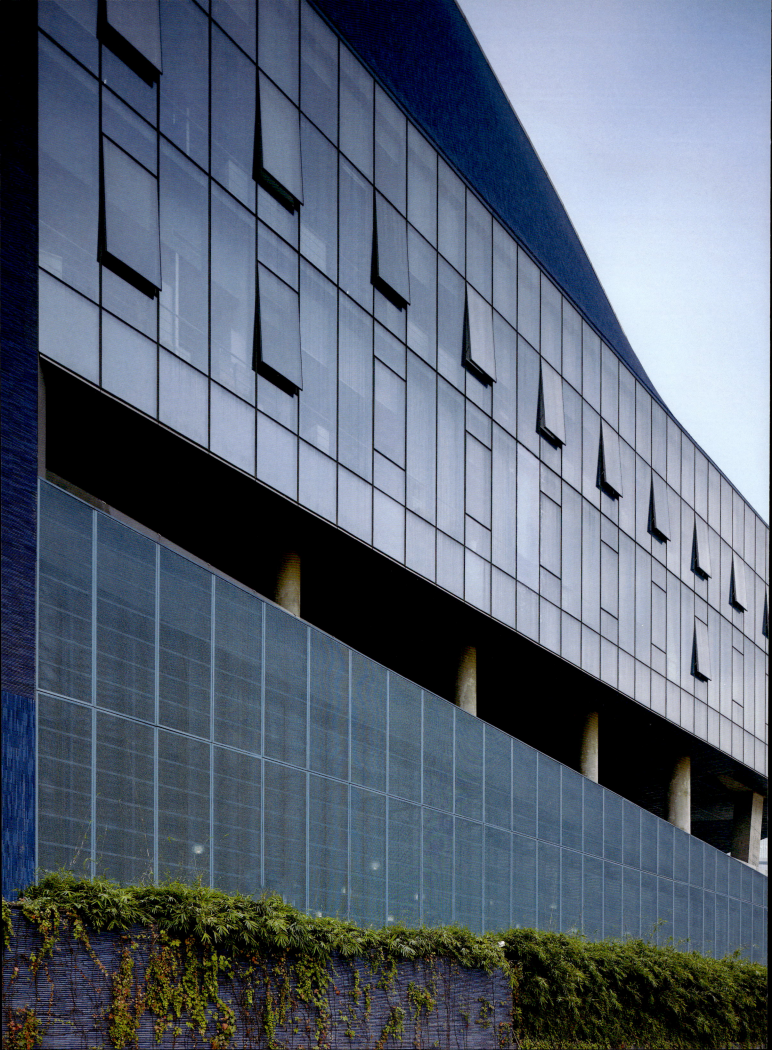

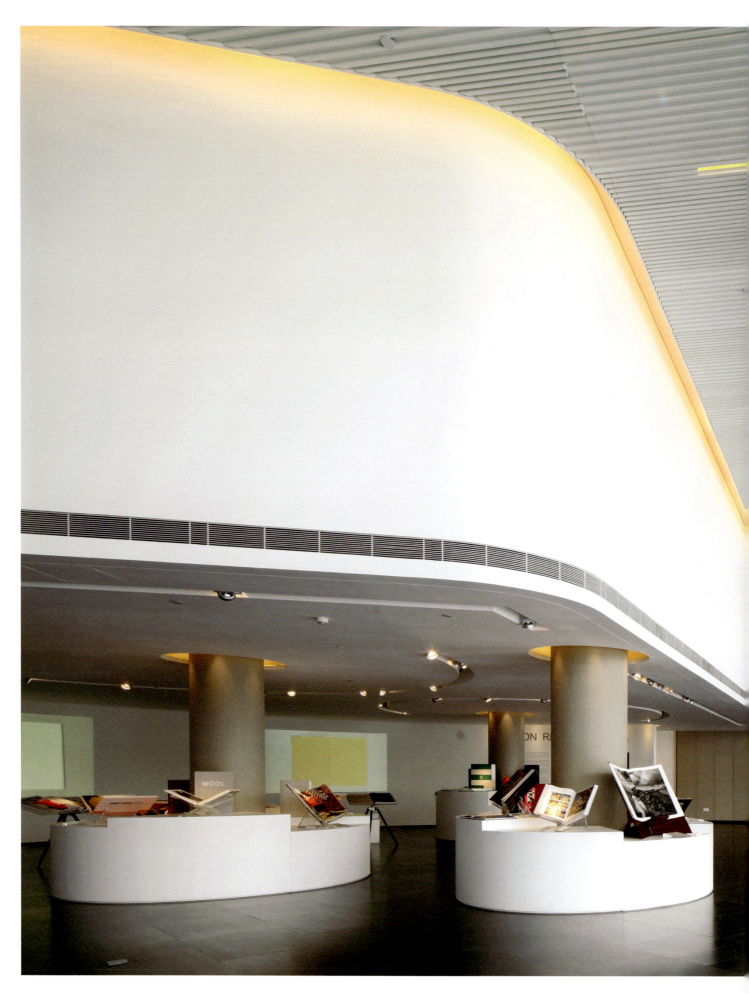

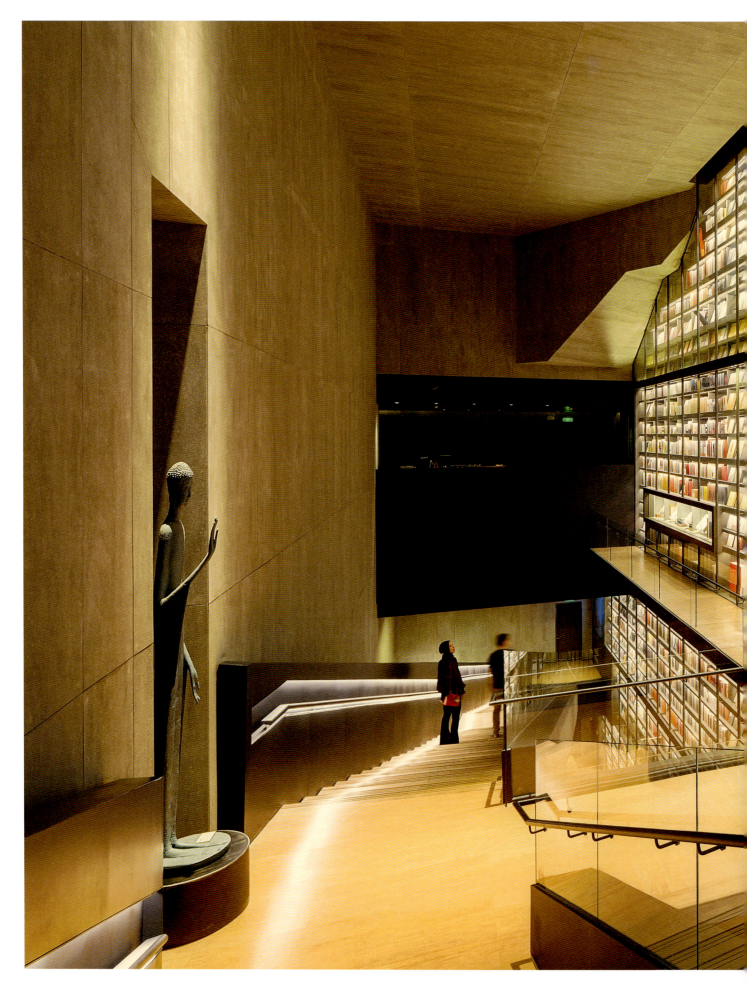

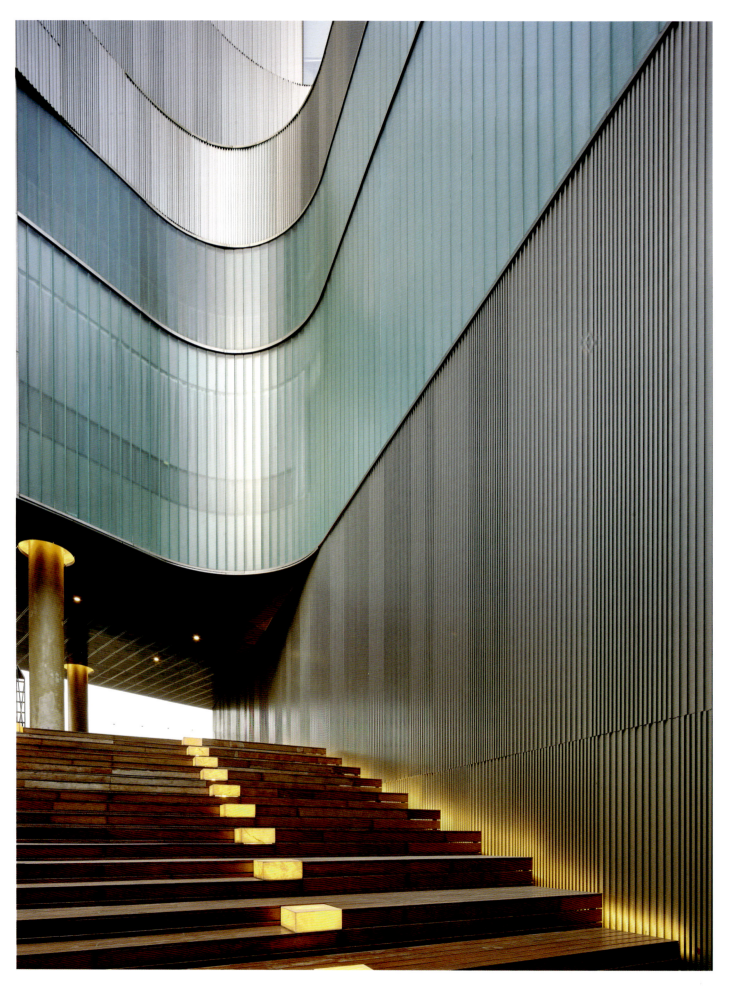

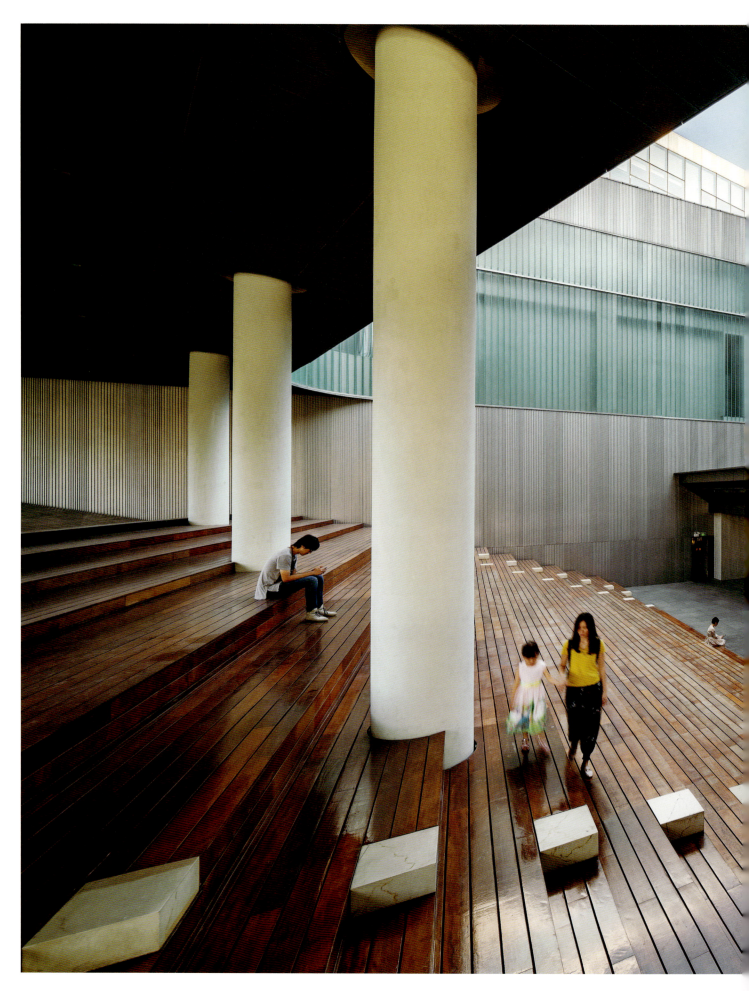

246 | THE BUILDING

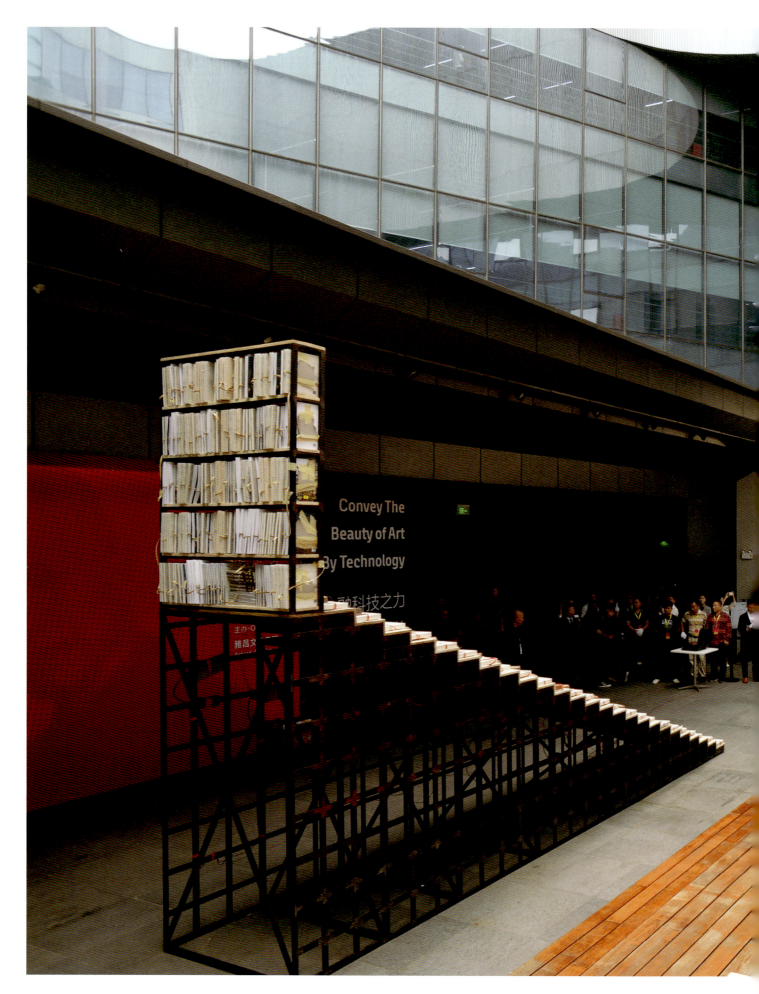

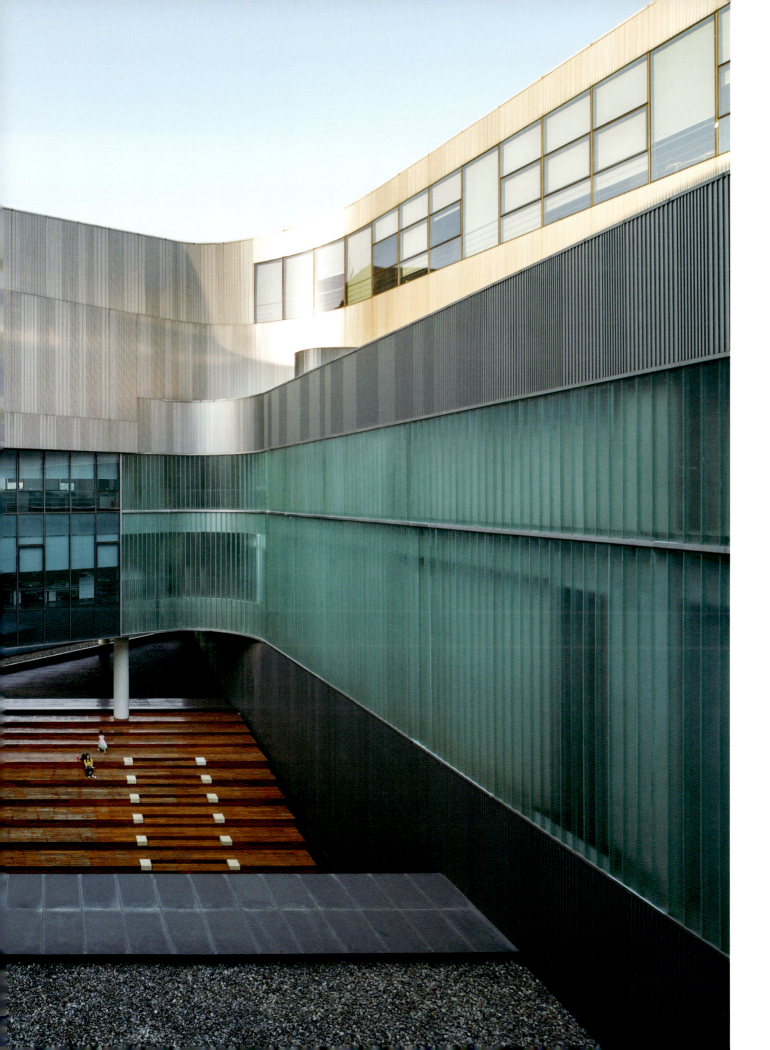

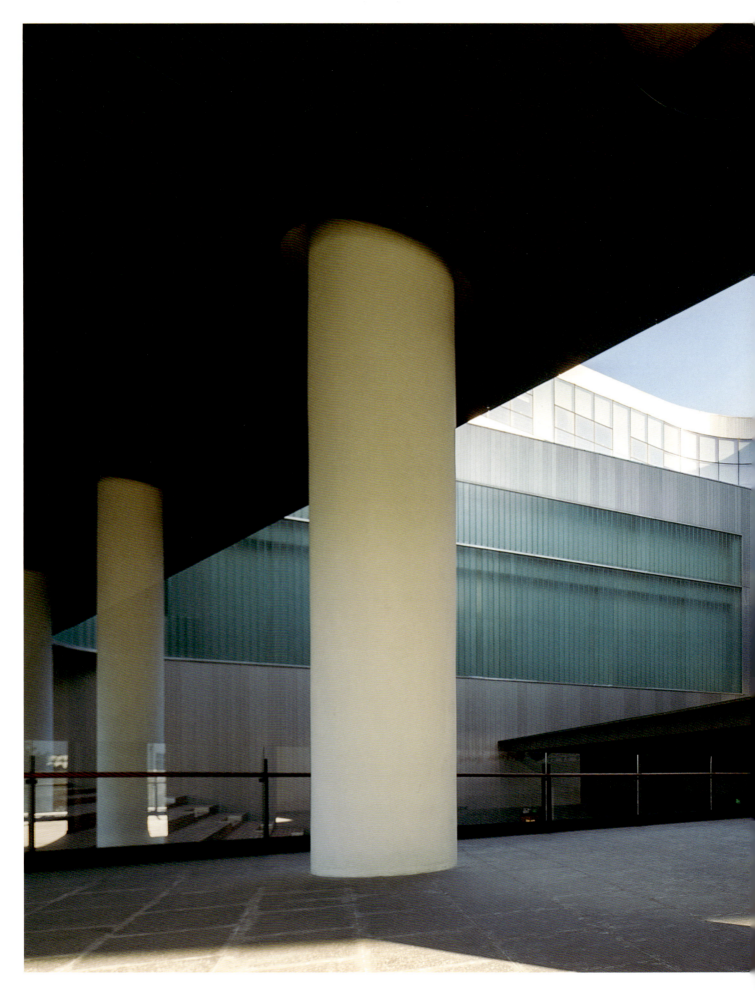

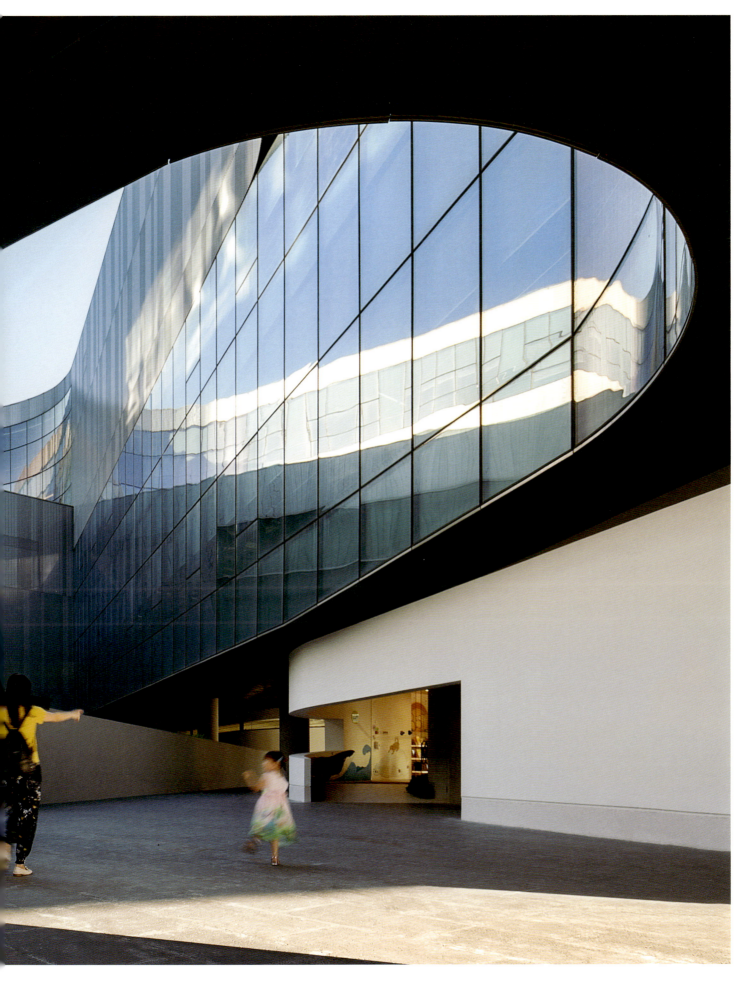

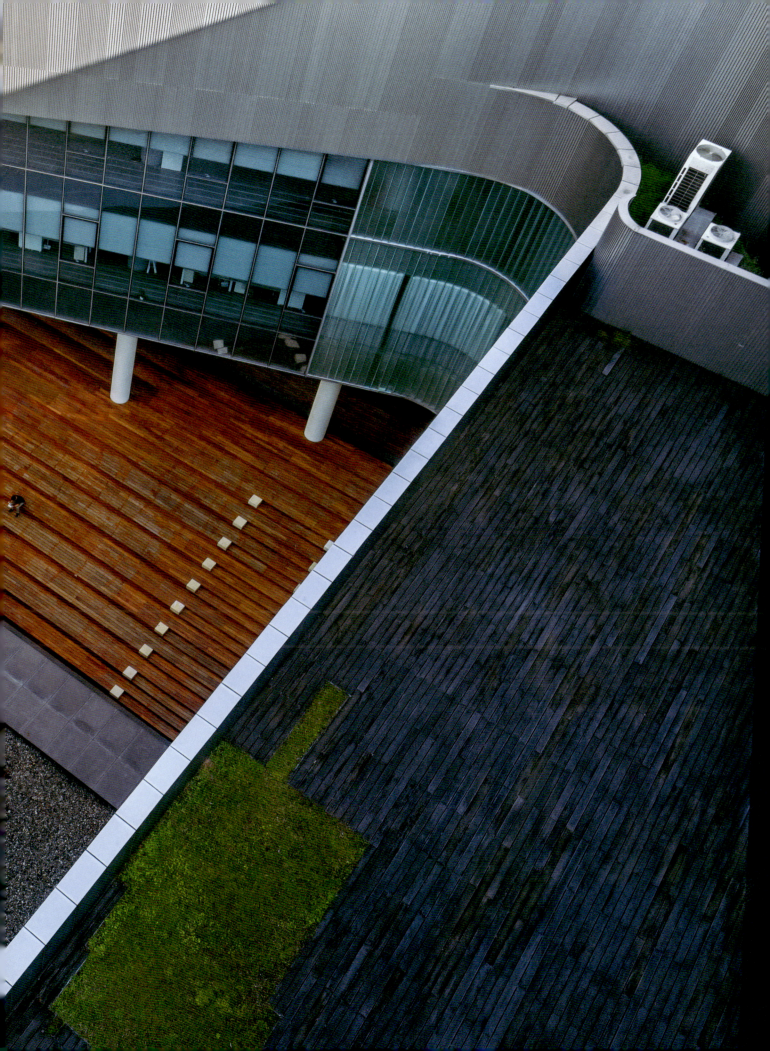

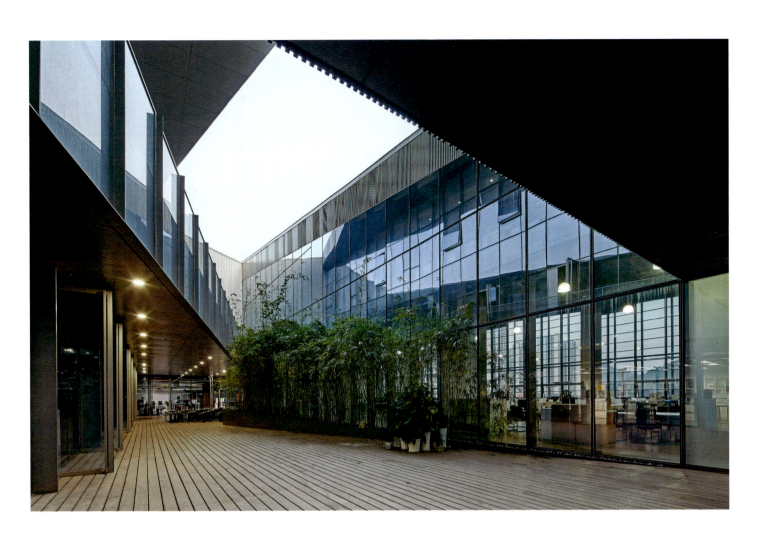

APPENDIX

BIOGRAPHY

Meng Yan
Principal Architect and Co-founder of URBANUS Architecture & Design Inc.

In 1999, MENG Yan co-founded URBANUS with partners LIU Xiaodu and WANG Hui. He has focused on architectural design and urban research in the context of contemporary Chinese cities for 20 years. As Principal in charge of Design of URBANUS, MENG Yan has led numerous design projects over the years. These projects have won an international reputation for URBANUS, including Luohu Art Gallery, Dafen Art Museum, the OCT Art & Design Gallery, OCT-LOFT Renovation, Tulou Collective Housing, Maillen Hotel & Apartment, Nanshan Marriage Registration Center, Artron Art Center, CGN Headquarters Building, Zhongdian Complex, the Southern University of Science and Technology library and gymnasium and recently completed SHUM YIP Upper-Hills LOFT, the Renovation of Meng Sheng Residence, etc. His works have been exhibited in international architectural exhibitions in New York, Berlin, Paris, Barcelona, Lisbon, Rotterdam, Tokyo and other places and have been published in academic journals.

MENG Yan's work has long focused on the key issues of China's urban development, including social and cultural issues of rapid urbanization, high-density urban building typologies, Urban Village regeneration and preservation of historical areas. He has led many urban design and research projects, such as a series of studies on Shenzhen's Urban Villages, including Nantou Old Town Preservation and Regeneration, Hubei Old Village and Baishizhou 5 Villages Urban Regeneration Research, Huaqiangbei Catic City Urban Design, as well as Preservation & Regeneration of Historic Qianmen East Hutong Area in Beijing, etc.

MENG Yan is an architect licensed in New York State and a RIBA Chartered Architect. He received his Bachelor's and Master's degrees of Architecture from Tsinghua University, and Master's degree of Architecture from Miami University. MENG Yan was a visiting professor at the School of Architecture in the University of Hong Kong and Syracuse University. He has been invited as a jury member for numerous international design competitions and to lecture at many international academic institutions. MENG Yan is one of the chief curators for 2017 Shenzhen-Hong Kong Bi-City Biennale of Urbanism/Architecture (Shenzhen) and the chief curator of the Shenzhen Pavilion in the 2010 Shanghai Expo.

PROJECT CREDITS

Principal Architect
Meng Yan

Location
Nanshan District, Shenzhen

Client
Artron Art (Group) Limited

Design
2008-2013

Construction
2010-2015

Site Area
12,535m²

Floor Area
41,504m²

Project Manager
Zhou Yalin

Project Architect
Rao Enchen (Architecture)
Wei Zhijiao (Landscape)

Project General Manager
Lin Haibin

Team
- Xiong Jiawei, Liang Guangfa, Wu Chunying, Ai Yun, Sun Yanhua, Huang Zhiyi, Chang Chen, Guo Jing, Xie Shengfen, Zhuang Jihong (Architecture)
- Lin Ting, Yu Xiaolan, Liu Jie, Chen Danping, Huang Chenhang (Landscape)
- Yao Dianbin, Xu Luoyi (Technical Director)
- Wang Weiyang (Internship)

Collaborators
- Wendell Burnette Architects (Interior Design)
- Artmost Design and Construction Co., Ltd. (Interior Design)
- Guangzhou RBS Architecture Engineer Design Associates (Structure)
- Shenzhen Tianyu Dynamo-electric Engineering Design Firm
- ECO Building Façade Technologies Ltd.

Photographers
Zeng Tianpei, Alex Chan, Wang Dayong, Wu Qiwei, Yang Chaoying

PHOTOGRAPHY CAPTIONS

West view facing street.
Photograph by ZtpVision.

2F courtyard.
Photograph by ©URBANUS.

Atrium archive.
Photograph by ZtpVision.

Artron night view from near highway.
Photograph by ZtpVision.

Bird's-eye night view.
Photograph by WANG Dayong.

Atrium archive.
Photograph by ©Artron.

Bird's-eye night view.
Photograph by WANG Dayong.

2F terrace façade.
Photograph by ZtpVision.

Courtyard.
Photograph by ©Artron.

Site top view.
Photograph by ©Google Maps.

Site photo.
Photograph by ©URBANUS.

Site Photo.
Photograph by ©URBANUS.

Site photo.
Photograph by ©URBANUS.

Construction materials.
Photograph by Oscar Riera Ojeda.

Construction materials.
Photograph by Oscar Riera Ojeda.

Construction materials.
Photograph by Oscar Riera Ojeda.

Construction materials.
Photograph by Oscar Riera Ojeda.

Construction materials.
Photograph by Oscar Riera Ojeda.

Construction site.
Photograph by Oscar Riera Ojeda.

Team photo at the construction site.
Photograph by ©Artron.

Construction site.
Photograph by Oscar Riera Ojeda.

Team photo at the construction site.
Photograph by Oscar Riera Ojeda.

Manufacturing area
(Under construction).
Photograph by Oscar Riera Ojeda.

Stairs at the atrium archive
(Under construction).
Photograph by Oscar Riera Ojeda.

Canteen (Under construction).
Photograph by Oscar Riera Ojeda.

Mezzanine floor
(Under construction).
Photograph by Oscar Riera Ojeda.

Mezzanine floor
(Under construction).
Photograph by Oscar Riera Ojeda.

Canteen (Under construction).
Photograph by Oscar Riera Ojeda.

Construction site.
Photograph by Oscar Riera Ojeda.

Bird's-eye view
(Under construction).
Photograph by ©Artron.

Bird's-eye view
(Under construction).
Photograph by ©Artron.

Bird's-eye view
(Under construction).
Photograph by ©Artron.

Construction site.
Photograph by Oscar Riera Ojeda.

Construction materials.
Photograph by Oscar Riera Ojeda.

Construction site.
Photograph by ©Artron.

Construction site.
Photograph by Oscar Riera Ojeda.

Construction site.
Photograph by ©Artron.

2F bookbinding
(Under construction).
Photograph by Oscar Riera Ojeda.

2F bookbinding
(Under construction).
Photograph by Oscar Riera Ojeda.

4F office courtyard
(Under construction).
Photograph by Oscar Riera Ojeda.

Construction site.
Photograph by Oscar Riera Ojeda.

Service stairs
(Under construction).
Photograph by Oscar Riera Ojeda.

Service stairs
(Under construction).
Photograph by Oscar Riera Ojeda.

Service stairs
(Under construction).
Photograph by Oscar Riera Ojeda.

Construction site.
Photograph by Oscar Riera Ojeda.

Construction site.
Photograph by Oscar Riera Ojeda.

Construction site.
Photograph by Oscar Riera Ojeda.

Construction site.
Photograph by ©URBANUS.

2F courtyard.
(Under construction).
Photograph by Oscar Riera Ojeda.

Construction site.
Photograph by ©Artron.

5F Terrace
(Under construction).
Photograph by ©URBANUS.

View of the mezzanine facing
courtyard (Under construction).
Photograph by ©URBANUS.

Canteen (Under construction).
Photograph by Oscar Riera Ojeda.

4F office (Under construction).
Photograph by Oscar Riera Ojeda.

Canteen (Under construction).
Photograph by Oscar Riera Ojeda.

2F bookbinding
(Under construction).
Photograph by Oscar Riera Ojeda.

2F (Under construction).
Photograph by Oscar Riera Ojeda.

2F terrace
(Under construction).
Photograph by Oscar Riera Ojeda.

Ceiling (Under construction).
Photograph by Oscar Riera Ojeda.

2F bookbinding
(Under construction).
Photograph by Oscar Riera Ojeda.

2F terrace
(Under construction).
Photograph by Oscar Riera Ojeda.

1F printing room
(Under construction).
Photograph by Oscar Riera Ojeda.

1F lobby
(Under construction).
Photograph by Oscar Riera Ojeda.

Canteen (Under construction).
Photograph by Oscar Riera Ojeda.

4F (Under construction).
Photograph by Oscar Riera Ojeda.

Gallery roof
(Under construction).
Photograph by Oscar Riera Ojeda.

URBANUS team at the
construction site.
Photograph by Oscar Riera Ojeda.

4F office
(Under construction).
Photograph by Oscar Riera Ojeda.

5F terrace
(Under construction).
Photograph by Oscar Riera Ojeda.

Construction materials.
Photograph by Oscar Riera Ojeda.

Atrium archive
(Under construction).
Photograph by Oscar Riera Ojeda.

4F office (Under construction).
Photograph by Oscar Riera Ojeda.

4F office courtyard.
Photograph by Oscar Riera Ojeda.

Bird's-eye view
(Under construction).
Photograph by ©Artron.

4F corner area
(Under construction).
Photograph by Oscar Riera Ojeda.

Courtyard
(Under construction).
Photograph by ©Artron.

4F office
(Under construction).
Photograph by Oscar Riera Ojeda.

Courtyard
(Under construction).
Photograph by Oscar Riera Ojeda.

4F office
(Under construction).
Photograph by Oscar Riera Ojeda.

6F office
(Under construction).
Photograph by Oscar Riera Ojeda.

Canteen (Under construction).
Photograph by Oscar Riera Ojeda.

View of canteen from mezzanine floor
(Under construction).
Photograph by Oscar Riera Ojeda.

Canteen (Under construction).
Photograph by Oscar Riera Ojeda.

Mezzanine floor
(Under construction).
Photograph by Oscar Riera Ojeda.

4F manufacture area
(Under construction).
Photograph by Oscar Riera Ojeda.

3F office
(Under construction).
Photograph by Oscar Riera Ojeda.

2F bookbinding
(Under construction).
Photograph by Oscar Riera Ojeda.

2F (Under construction).
Photograph by Oscar Riera Ojeda.

2F bookbinding
(Under construction).
Photograph by Oscar Riera Ojeda.

Atrium archive
(Under construction).
Photograph by Oscar Riera Ojeda.

1F atrium archive
(Under construction).
Photograph by Oscar Riera Ojeda.

5F Gallery
(Under construction).
Photograph by Oscar Riera Ojeda.

5F Gallery
(Under construction).
Photograph by Oscar Riera Ojeda.

5F Gallery
(Under construction).
Photograph by Oscar Riera Ojeda.

Construction Site.
Photograph by Oscar Riera Ojeda.

Traffic Core
(Under construction).
Photograph by ©Artron.

5F gallery
(Under construction).
Photograph by Oscar Riera Ojeda.

Stairs (Under construction).
Photograph by Oscar Riera Ojeda.

5F gallery
(Under construction).
Photograph by Oscar Riera Ojeda.

Ceiling (Under construction).
Photograph by Oscar Riera Ojeda.

Column (Under construction).
Photograph by Oscar Riera Ojeda.

5F gallery
(Under construction).
Photograph by Oscar Riera Ojeda.

5F terrace
(Under construction).
Photograph by ©Artron.

Courtyard (Under construction).
Photograph by Oscar Riera Ojeda.

Courtyard
(Under construction).
Photograph by Oscar Riera Ojeda.

2F terrace
(Under construction)
Photograph by Oscar Riera Ojeda.

5F gallery
(Under construction).
Photograph by WU Qiwei.

5F gallery
(Under construction).
Photograph by WU Qiwei.

5F gallery
(Under construction).
Photograph by WU Qiwei.

5F gallery
(Under construction).
Photograph by WU Qiwei.

5F gallery
(Under construction).
Photograph by WU Qiwei.

2F terrace
(Under construction).
Photograph by WU Qiwei.

Courtyard
(Under construction).
Photograph by WU Qiwei.

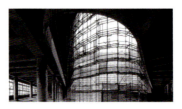

2F terrace
(Under construction).
Photograph by WU Qiwei.

Courtyard
(Under construction).
Photograph by WU Qiwei.

Courtyard
(Under construction).
Photograph by WU Qiwei.

2F terrace
(Under construction).
Photograph by WU Qiwei.

Roof construction
(Under construction).
Photograph by Alex Chan.

Roof construction
(Under construction).
Photograph by Alex Chan.

5f Cooling Tower-Outdoor
Equipment Area
(Under construction).
Photograph by Alex Chan.

Roof construction.
Photograph by Alex Chan.

5F gallery
(Under construction).
Photograph by Alex Chan.

5F terrace
(Under construction).
Photograph by Alex Chan.

Chairman office & gallery façade
(Under construction).
Photograph by Alex Chan.

Chairman office & gallery façade
(Under construction).
Photograph by Alex Chan.

Atrium archive exterior façade
(Under construction).
Photograph by Alex Chan.

2F terrace
(Under construction).
Photograph by Alex Chan.

4F office courtyard
(Under construction).
Photograph by Alex Chan.

5F gallery
(Under construction).
Photograph by Alex Chan.

5F gallery
(Under construction).
Photograph by Alex Chan.

Atrium archive
(Under construction).
Photograph by Oscar Riera Ojeda.

Atrium archive
(Under construction).
Photograph by WU Qiwei.

Atrium archive
(Under construction)
Photograph by Oscar Riera Ojeda.

Atrium archive
(Under construction).
Photograph by Oscar Riera Ojeda.

Atrium archive
(Under construction).
Photograph by Alex Chan.

Atrium archive
(Under construction).
Photograph by Alex Chan.

Atrium archive
(Under construction).
Photograph by Alex Chan.

Atrium archive
(Under construction).
Photograph by Alex Chan.

Atrium archive
(Under construction).
Photograph by Alex Chan.

4F office
(Under construction).
Photograph by Alex Chan.

6F office
(Under construction)
Photograph by Alex Chan.

3F office
(Under construction).
Photograph by Alex Chan.

1F lobby
(Under construction).
Photograph by Alex Chan.

3F office
(Under construction).
Photograph by Alex Chan.

5F gallery
(Under construction).
Photograph by Alex Chan.

2F terrace
(Under construction).
Photograph by Alex Chan.

4F office courtyard
(Under construction).
Photograph by Alex Chan.

2F terrace
(Under construction).
Photograph by Alex Chan.

Exterior view facing street
(Under construction).
Photograph by Alex Chan.

General aerial view.
Photograph by WANG Dayong.

General aerial view.
Photograph by WANG Dayong.

General aerial view.
Photograph by WANG Dayong.

General aerial view.
Photograph by ZtpVision.

Exterior view facing street.
Photograph by YANG Chaoying.

Exterior façade.
Photograph by YANG Chaoying.

Exterior façade.
Photograph by WANG Dayong.

General aerial view.
Photograph by ©Artron Chen Yu.

Exterior façade.
Photograph by YANG Chaoying.

Exterior view facing street.
Photograph by ZtpVision.

Exterior view facing street.
Photograph by YANG Chaoying.

Exterior façade.
Photograph by YANG Chaoying.

West view facing street.
Photograph by ZtpVision.

South elevation.
Photograph by YANG Chaoying.

Exterior façade.
Photograph by YANG Chaoying.

1F lobby.
Photograph by Alex Chan.

1F lobby.
Photograph by Alex Chan.

1F lobby.
Photograph by Alex Chan.

Atrium archive.
Photograph by Alex Chan.

Atrium archive.
Photograph by

Atrium archive.
Photograph by ZtpVision.

Atrium archive.
Photograph by ©Artron.

Atrium archive.
Photograph by ©Artron Zou Jia.

Atrium archive.
Photograph by ©URBANUS.

Atrium archive.
Photograph by Alex Chan.

Atrium archive.
Photograph by ZtpVision.

Atrium archive.
Photograph by ZtpVision.

2F terrace.
Photograph by ZtpVision.

The large staircase connecting the 2f terrace and mezzanine floor.
Photograph by YANG Chaoying.

2F terrace.
Photograph by YANG Chaoying.

The large staircase connecting the 2F terrace and mezzanine floor.
Photograph by YANG Chaoying.

The large staircase connecting the 2F terrace and mezzanine floor.
Photograph by ZtpVision.

2F courtyard.
Photograph by ZtpVision.

The large staircase connecting the 2F terrace and mezzanine floor.
Photograph by ©Artron Chen Yu.

The large staircase connecting the 2F terrace and mezzanine floor.
Photograph by ©Artron Zou Jia.

The large staircase connecting the 2F terrace and mezzanine floor.
Photograph by ©Artron Chen Yu.

Courtyard.
Photograph by ZtpVision.

2F courtyard.
Photograph by ©URBANUS.

2F courtyard.
Photograph by ©URBANUS.

2F courtyard.
Photograph by ©Artron Zou Jia.

Courtyard.
Photograph by ©Artron.

Courtyard.
Photograph by ©Artron.

2F courtyard.
Photograph by ZtpVision.

2F terrace.
Photograph by ZtpVision.

2F terrace.
Photograph by ZtpVision.

2F terrace.
Photograph by ZtpVision.

2F courtyard.
Photograph by ZtpVision.

Office.
Photograph by ©Artron.

Canteen.
Photograph by Alex Chan.

4F Office Courtyard.
Photograph by ZtpVision.

4F office courtyard.
Photograph by ZtpVision.

4F office courtyard.
Photograph by YANG Chaoying.

4F office.
Photograph by Alex Chan.

5F gallery balcony.
Photograph by ZtpVision.

5F gallery balcony.
Photograph by ZtpVision.

5F gallery.
Photograph by ©Artron Zou Jia.

5F gallery.
Photograph by ©Artron Chen Yu.

5F gallery.
Photograph by ©Artron Zou Jia.

5F exhibition space.
Photograph by Alex Chan.

5F exhibition space.
Photograph by ©Artron.

5F stairs to the chairman's office.
Photograph by ©Artron.

5F stairs to the chairman office.
Photograph by Alex Chan.

5F stairs to the chairman's office.
Photograph by ©Artron.

5F exhibition space.
Photograph by ©Artron.

6F office.
Photograph by Alex Chan.

6F office.
Photograph by Alex Chan.

5F terrace.
Photograph by ZtpVision.

Service stairs.
Photograph by Alex Chan.

Service stairs.
Photograph by ©URBANUS.

1F printing room.
Photograph by Alex Chan.

1F printing room.
Photograph by ©Artron Zou Jia.

1F printing room.
Photograph by ©Artron Zou Jia.

1F printing room.
Photograph by Alex Chan.

Exterior façade.
Photograph by ZtpVision.

5F terrace.
Photograph by Alex Chan.

BOOK CREDITS

Book Layout by Lucía B Bauzá & Ana Viana.
Art Direction by Oscar Riera Ojeda.
Copy Editing by Kit Maude & Michael W. Phillips Jr.

OSCAR RIERA OJEDA
PUBLISHERS

Copyright © 2022 by Oscar Riera Ojeda Publishers Limited
ISBN 978-1-946226-39-6
Published by Oscar Riera Ojeda Publishers Limited
Printed in China by Artron Art Group
This book is possible with the generous contribution of the Artron Art Group.

Oscar Riera Ojeda Publishers Limited
Unit 1003-04, 10/F.,
Shanghai Industrial Investment Building,
48-62 Hennessy Road, Wanchai, Hong Kong
T: +852-3920-9300

Production Offices | China
Suit 19, Shenyun Road,
Nanshan District, Shenzhen 518055
T:+1-484-502-5400

www.oropublishers.com | www.oscarrieraojeda.com
oscar@oscarrieraojeda.com